Whispers of Passion

By

J. Albines

The Passionate Journey

1) **Riding Free** – A woman finds freedom after her divorce, and returns to one of her first true loves. ***Pg. 5***

2) **The Toronto Subway** – A story of woman empowerment. She had grown tired of the eyes that judged her, and took hold of the power that had always been available to her. ***Pg. 10***

3) **Saddle Up** – The two passions in her life were horses and her husband. But, it wasn't until Sadie rode into her life, that true passion was awakened. ***Pg. 27***

4) **In The Shadows** – She spent her life thinking she was crazy. The man in the shadows controlled her every thought, her every desire. But, she knew, he was just a figment of her imagination - till she felt his teeth upon her neck. ***Pg. 41***

5) **The Pittsburgh Estate** – She was the proverbial fly on the wall, seen but generally ignored. Her desire to be one of the women behind her boss's door, screaming in ecstasy, finally pulled her out of her shell. *Pg. 75*

6) **A Little Wine On Ice** – Tired of feeling like everyone else's life was better, it was time to change things up. But, what could possibly happen at a winery with friends. *Pg. 97*

7) **By The Light Of The Moon** – Johanna moves into a warehouse district, to escape her life, and work on her art. She finds herself infatuated with the man across the street. Although she fears the night, she follows him. *Pg. 127*

8) **The White Knight** – Her world was crashing down around her, and there seemed to be no end in sight. As she sat in the weeds, on the side of the road, love would find her. *Pg. 161*

9) **The Affair** – The divorce ripped everything from her, everything she had worked for. She jumped into one bad relationship after another. Then, something was

awakened within her, and her journey began. While trying to find herself, she would end up finding her passion, and taking others along for the ride. *Pg. 199*

10) **The River** – As a woman who had spent much of her life in control, Adrienne found herself surrendering to her need to be out of control. She boarded a river barge on a journey down river, and from there the fantasy would write itself. *Pg. 300*

11) **Poems –** *Pg. 347*

Feeling Free

It was a 2001 Harley Davidson Heritage, but it was much more than that - it was a new her. She had ridden motorcycles, on and off, since she was six years old; but, set that passion aside for family. That was all behind her now. She couldn't wait to test drive it, and he was more than willing to let her have it inspected before she bought it. She was going to anyway; it was just a matter of going through the motions. Its slick red and black paint called to her. Its shiny, reflective, chrome covered parts, mesmerized her. She was off without hesitation.

By the time she arrived at the dealership, she was beside herself. She wasn't thinking like her old self; cautious, guarded, and controlled. Perhaps it was the excitement. Perhaps it was the freedom. Perhaps, it was the historic vibration of the Harley Davidson between her legs. She felt free; felt alive; felt excited; felt beautiful; desired; erotic; powerful; euphoric; felt all of these at once. When the technician approached, she knew she was in trouble. He was tall, handsome, confident in his stance, and his eyes made her heart flutter. His chiseled facial features concealed slightly, with a neatly trimmed beard - just enough scruff to unnerve her a bit.

His shirt was open at the top, buttons hanging, pulling the shirt to the side. She could see the arch of his chest, the muscle tight against the skin. She had difficulty speaking, answering his questions; not even catching his name. She stood by, watching him run his rough, textured, hands down the bike. She could feel it. Removing the seat, he pinched his finger. Putting the corner of the thumb to his lips, she watched his tongue touch it. She could taste it. Her breathing began to shallow and become rapid, as her heartbeat quickened. He motioned her over, as he squared down beside the bike. He rattled off words, but she couldn't hear them. He pointed to the parts, but she couldn't see them. Her eyes were locked on his. She wasn't herself. Words faded in and out; "seat", "screw guide", "front intake", "pump drive", "piston stroke", "shaft." The whole time she had squatted beside him, she had not taken her eyes off him. His pants tight from squatting - his bulge pronounced! Her heart was beating faster. She could hear his deep voice ringing in her head. She placed her hand on his upper thigh and squeezed slightly. "Tell me again, what the shaft goes into!"

He paused and looked at her. "Let me show you!"

In the tool room, nearby, he closed the door behind them. With his left hand, he gripped her by the hair, pulling her back; his right hand around her throat. He could feel the throb of her heartbeat. He ran his thumb across her lips, arousing the nerves that were going numb. Their lips finding each other so easily. Their tongues were in perfect harmony with each other's wants. She was still wearing her nursing scrubs from work. They were loose, and effortlessly gave way to the pull of his hands.

 Up onto the work table, he lifted her. Her legs spread without a single word. His lips, then his beard, tickled her inner thighs. She could wait no longer, the tease too much. "Oh God!..........

Oh God!" She gripped his hair pulling him in. His lips, his tongue, gentle in their trade. The pressure in her chest just seemed too much. His hot breath, between her legs, made her throat feel like it was closing in. Her breaths were getting shorter. The feeling of excitement so vivid and real, it was almost painful and unbearable. "Oh God! Oh My God!" She breathed deep. Her head back, trying to catch her breath. She cried out, "I want you inside me!"

He grabbed her behind the knees, sliding her across the table towards him. Pulling her head back, he cupped his mouth along her neck, just enough suction to cause her chest to fill with air. He cradled her breast in his still greasy hand and consumed her nipple whole. She gasped. She tensed, pulling on his shoulders. The firmness of his muscles gave her little to grip onto. Her nipples hardened. His slight nibbling, making her face feel weightless, drained of its blood. She gasped for air. His pants undone, he pulled her down. She could feel it thicken filling her mouth. She could feel it swell. It forced her jaws open. He wouldn't let her finish. She held him, his size filling her hand in a hard erect posture. He turned her, the wrenches and drawers rattling, as he pushed up against the tool chest. He probed her with his fingers. She was moist from his lips; her senses fully awake from his circling tongue. She was ready.

She screamed out as he answered her throbbing plea between her legs, stretching her! He grabbed her by the throat, squeezing lightly. "Shhhhh!" He covered her mouth, muffling her cries at each thrust of his hips. Deep, he penetrated! She no longer knew where she was; oblivious to the ringing of the tools, the rattle of the cabinet drawers, and the pounding against the wall.

Her legs weakened at each thrust; his strength taking hers; her knees giving way, her legs collapsing beneath her. He picked her up, spreading her wider, taking it deeper. She screamed, but could not hear her own voice. She just clenched him. Holding on after he was done, not wanting to lose the sensation.

As she walked from the tool room, she tossed her disheveled hair, and tugged on her outfit, both in disarray. She walked past the manager. "I'll take it!"

The Toronto Subway

She never missed a chance to go to the Toronto Performing Arts Centre in North York. This meeting, however, was unproductive, and had run later than planned. After work, she was to meet with friends; live a little; let go of the burdens that had been weighing heavy on her shoulders; to put herself back in control of her life. As a television producer, many would think that she was always in control, but it was the furthest thing from the truth. Her primary responsibility was that of a crises manager; juggler; bender of rules when no one was looking; accommodator of needs to accomplish the goal. So, here she was, sacrificing that freedom for the sake of work once again. Where was the freedom in that? She had worn one of her favorite outfits, just for this occasion. It made her feel sexy; made her feel feminine; made her feel desirable – it was work and play, all sewn up into one. One concealed under the other. There was an anxiety that had been building within her, rearing its ugly head when society's restrictions made her feel boxed in. Or, maybe they were self-imposed restrictions that she placed on herself – always concerned how others would see her or judge her. Up to this point, she had dedicated her life to her career, and a marriage that ultimately failed. Her priorities were changing. She wanted to feel completely free, free from restriction, free from her own inhibitions.

When she entered at the North York Centre, the Toronto Subway Car was scarcely occupied. The midnight hour may have worried her, but the few occupants were a scattered bunch of middle aged men – harmless business looking type gentleman. She was keenly aware of their eyes upon her; watching her; dreaming of her; fantasies rolling through their heads. The attention was gratifying to her, but annoyed her at the same time. How free they must feel to just stare at her without concern. How in control they must feel to push her feelings aside, to satisfy their own lustful thoughts. How powerful they are to control her movements in such a way; Her legs to be crossed so as not to appear too promiscuous; Her eyes to look elsewhere, or she would most certainly lose the staring match. How uncomfortable that power over her, made her feel. She wanted control. She wanted back the power they were taking from her. But, it also made her feel beautiful. She stood up, throwing her long coat on the bench. Her skirt rose up slightly from the draft, revealing the muscular tone of her legs. A loose fitting black skirt, clipped on at the waist, concealing her other outfit underneath; the one she wore to meet with friends – a night to let loose, and be free. She was feeling the music, the beat, the rhythm in her head; feeling the moment. It was one of those moments that she couldn't define. Where the music was coming from, she could no longer tell; maybe in her head; maybe from somewhere else – it didn't matter. Placing her foot on the seat, with her four (4) inch heel pressed hard against the curve in the seat, her leg was tense. Her skirt fell to the side as she pushed it up her thigh towards her hip. For a moment, she paused, looking at her thigh, running her fingers down the upper seam of her pantyhose. All eyes were on her. She smiled to herself, and breathed deep; her chest rising, flipping her hair back. "Just do it!" she thought to herself. "Be free!" Already, she was throwing her cares aside. Slowly, she pushed the stockings down her leg, and unfastened the strap of her shoe to remove it. She placed her other hand on the pole beside her, her red nails highlighted on the chrome pole. Leaning over slightly, she removed her shoe; delicately she ran a finger down along her ankle and foot, pushing her hose off. She could hear the men watching release the air from their lungs, as if they had been holding it from the moment she stepped on. Slipping her shoe back on, she looked at the men through her long blonde hair. This was her production, and there was no doubt she had her audience's attention.

When she pulled her skirt up, to explore her other thigh, she again slipped her fingers underneath the edge of the hose. The men breathed in, almost in unison. A long slow torture followed. Each of them hesitant to get off at their stop, a few missing theirs, so all but a few remained. She looked down the length of the almost empty car; its bright red seats; its chrome hand rails scattered throughout the car. It's scuffed up grey dance floor. The light coming in through the windows flashing off the shiny rails, bars lining the seats, bars standing erect to be stroked repeatedly, hanging from the ceiling to be handled and gripped tightly. Those flickering lights from outside the train, bouncing off each of these like the lights of a camera. She gripped the pole and turned to her audience. The feeling of being desired was invigorating to her. They couldn't even look away when she looked them in the eyes. Turning, she placed her back against the pole, and unclasped her skirt letting it fall to the floor. She tugged at her blouse, unfastening each button from its hole, and let it slide down her arms as she lifted herself off the pole, arching her back slightly. Underneath, she wore her one piece, form fitting, V-neck, long sleeve, body suit. Clinging to her body like it was painted on, it melted into her curves so well that no man or woman could help but desire to touch her; to feel her; to taste her; to have her. Standing straight, her legs slightly apart, as your eyes followed up the lines of her legs, they curved up and in from the knee. There they lightly touched mid thigh. Every man's eyes wanting to be fingers if only to touch that skin but once. When the thighs parted way again, they continued upward, and inward, creating a valley of such beauty that you could lose yourself in it for an eternity. Shaped like a diamond, this valley only guarded by a thin layer of red velvety cloth. That cloth, soft and thin, wrapped itself around the slightest of curves, accentuating the soft structure of her pleasure with masterful skill and artistry. The cuff, of the all but non-existent pant leg, crept up into that valley, the material itself wanting to be closer to its beauty. The curve of her perfectly formed thighs pushed the material upward and inward; wanting it closer; wanting it tighter. She could feel its pressure against her most sensitive areas; keeping her aroused all day; pressing against her pleasure each time she leaned forward, making the material even tighter. Only the wrinkles were left desiring more, as the cloth stretched, and spread, material filling in her most valuable of crevices. Her hips rounded like the curve of the earth, holding the perfect womb, reaching up to its inward peak where the lower ribs curve inward. This is how she felt. This is how she saw herself. The material ran tight across her shoulders, and down the curvature of her breasts. The V-neck was deep down to the middle of the abdomen. The curve of her breasts half exposed, calling for attention. Her breasts were firm, pulling the skin tight. Poking through the cloth, her nipples showed their presence along the tight edge of the V, as it dropped downward. With her lips parted, and her large, round, brown eyes relaxed, eye lids resting part way down; you could tell she was feeling very beautiful and sexual. She felt alive!

At the far end of the car, amongst the few scattered older men, there sat one who stood out from the rest. He was probably an attorney, whose case had run late; or, maybe a business executive who spent more time at work than he did at home. His black hair slicked back, a prominent five o'clock shadow showing that he was at the end of a very long day. There was a strong bone structure evident in his frame. His lean face giving notice of his physical nature, cheeks sunken in slightly, eyes a penetrating blue. She was definitely taken with him, locking eyes with him. Popping her chin up, and her head back slightly, she signaled him to come to her. Tossing his suit jacket on the seat beside him, he stood. His collared white dress shirt was tight against his chest and arms. Loosely hanging around his neck, his tie, rest in the valley between the muscles of his chest. He walked slowly to her, with her watching his gait, his package shifting slightly at each step. As he stepped within feet of her, she stepped forward, covering his mouth. Shaking her head "No", she let him know that number one rule. Her hand falling to rest on his chest, its firm slopes, its strong ability to move whatever it needed, its dominant power. She could feel his hands closing in around her hips, making their way around the curves of her buttocks, so statuesque in their form. She spun around, taking control of his hands. Sliding the fingers of his right hand between her legs, she received no resistance from him. The music was still playing in her head, and her passion was keeping with the beat. With her eyes closed, she ran his left hand up the front of her body, placing his first two fingers into her mouth. She sucked on the fingers, as the pressure built between her legs. Breathing deep, her chest raised, she slid his hand down between her breasts and under her suit. As he squeezed, she gasped for air – and her audience did too. Removing his hand out from under her top, she placed it on the upright chrome rail, closing his fingers around the pole. Placing his right hand on the rail, she slid his tie off from around his neck, wrapping it around his hands and the pole.

Turning to face him, his arms at shoulder level, she ran her hands down the length of his arms, feeling their strength; their size; their power surrounding her. Across his shoulders her hands moved, meeting near the neck, where they began the task of unbuttoning his shirt. His skin was soft and arousing to touch. She mapped out his nipples and the curves of his upper body, with her fingers. Down the muscles of his abdomen, and around his sides to his lower back, she continued to explore. Her soft lips hardened his nipples. Her teeth feeling their stiffness, as she nibbled at them. As she ran her fingers up the middle of his back, along the muscle trail surrounding his spine, she clamped her teeth down onto his clavicle – arousing a shocked exhalation at once. Ducking underneath his arm, she pushed his hips towards the bench, seating him, and then forcing him to lie down. His hands still tied, he slid them down and around the pole, to lay down where he was directed. As he pulled, his tie began to loosen. She stopped the tie from unraveling further, looked at the man on the bench and shook her head "No!" She then placed her four inch heel against his cheek, covering his mouth with the arch of her sole. She retied the tie. Looking in his eyes, she didn't get the sense that he liked the taste of leather. Placing her hands on his stomach, her weight upon his abdominal muscles, her fingers rested comfortably between the ripples as he tensed from the added weight. Her heels poked him in the head as she squeezed her legs onto the bench alongside him. Her one piece suit, pulled tight and upward, between her legs. She sat upon his face, muffling his groans. The audience shifted in their seat. Through the velvety cloth, the hardness of his teeth pressed against her pleasure, his nose tickling her back door. She pressed against him harder.

Sliding her hands down his abdomen, she placed her tongue in his belly button, caressing its borders with her lips. She rose up, grinding her hips down against his jaw line. The crotch of his slacks rising up as she moved her hips back and forth, beginning to pull at the belt line. She hastened to answer its call, unlocking the belt, she unlatched the door. He wore no undergarments. His member was free and enlarged. Peeling back the folds of his pants, she pulled the zipper down. As she looked upon his size, she pressed her hips down hard into his face. Wrapping her hand around his girth, she raised it up, taking its tip between her lips. With slight suction, she released it with a loud kiss. She brought her lips to rest on his throbbing member, while she moved her hands down his pants legs. She allowed her fingers to explore the soft, curly, hair covering his thighs. Bringing her hands back up, she cupped his testicles in her hand; caressing the soft hairless skin – he was groomed!

Taking it in her hand again, she moved so that she was now straddling his legs. As she lowered her head, she gazed upon her audience. Her eyes remained on them, as she ran her tongue the length of his shaft. She watched the men adjust themselves, and lick their lips, as she tickled the tip – flicking it with her tongue. She wrapped her mouth around the head of that shaft, pulling on its position of power; through suction, her lips clinging on. The mouths of her audience dropping open through involuntary response. She smiled, clenching her teeth down lightly around his smooth skinned tip. Each member of her audience, with their hand between their legs, took a deep breath. Pulling her top apart, her breasts fell upon the eyes of wanting men. She pulled her arms from the sleeves, and they were hypnotized by the rocking back and forth. As she stood, her fingers elegantly slipped between the velvet cloth and her own succulent skin. She slowly pushed the material down her hips, exposing the beauty of her arching slopes. The flickering lights passing by the windows, adding shadow and excitement to the show. Down her legs, her one piece outfit slid, softly lowering to the ground. She straddled him once again, this time placing her hips over his. Her flowering passion pressed its lips against his swollen member; stroking his shaft; wrapping itself lightly around its muscle and strength. Leaning forward, she placed her nipple between his lips. Pulling on his ear to get him in line, putting his teeth in motion; she ordered him to suck the life from the breast till she said "no more" - then the other breast. With her hips lifted, she grasped his erect and hardened nature, placing the head between her lower lips. Back and forth, she moved it. Back and forth, with slight penetration, she pushed it. Pulling it out again, she ran her tongue the length of the shaft. From his lower region to his neck, she explored his body with her tongue and lips. All his muscles were tense and ready to pounce. She bit his lower lip.

Pushing his feet to the floor, she stepped aside. She turned her back to him, arching her back slightly. She knew she had teased him long enough. He rolled off the bench, pulling at the tie with his teeth, to loosen it. When he was free, he grabbed her by the hips, pushing her against the rail; spreading her diamond with his wanting aggression; drilling;

chipping away; resizing its accustomed capacity. It hurt. It hurt deep. It hurt wide. No other pain brought this much pleasure. He thrust. He spread. He penetrated. She felt each and every one of them. She turned, bending his member, ordering him down. Yanking his shirt down, free from his body, she pushed him back onto the bench. Wrapping his shirt around his neck, she then tied it to the back rail. Sliding his pants down to his feet, she marveled at how beautiful this man was. His physique perfectly in tune; where one muscle fades back into hiding, another emerges. His body was poetry in motion, each movement causing a rise in emotion. She ran her hands up the ankles, over the knees. As her fingers reached the muscled thighs, she pushed her finger tips down, feeling their tightness as she moved up his legs. She took his fully erect wanting probe into her hand, stroking it as she pulled up. Her lips tickling his inner thigh, finding their way between the thigh and the soft skinned sack that held the juice of life, she so desperately craved. Taking one in her mouth, it was now hers. On her tongue, she could feel it almost shrink in fear, surrender to her mercy. Once again, she ran her tongue up its length, looking into his eyes till she reached its tip. There, she consumed it; devouring it before the eyes of those watching. Deep in her throat, she held it, feeling it expand as he flexed it, while running her hands up and gripping the muscles of his chest. She lifted up, grabbing him by the hair, sticking her hardened nipple into his mouth. While he sucked, and massaged it in all its glory, she reached down, grabbing his dick, the tip pushing between the soft skin, her swollen needy lips, till it found its mark. Down upon it she slid, feeling that girth once again; feeling her skin spread at his thickness; feeling it probe deep within her. She gripped his hair tighter, pushing her breasts against him harder. Her legs felt weak, and her stomach tightened, each time she pushed down upon him. His size seemed overwhelming from the tightness of her body, for having been without for so long. It was a glorious pain, an indescribable euphoria of pain and ecstasy in one. She pulled his head backward, placing her other breast into his begging lips. Again, and again, she slid herself up and down, forward and backward. She rode him, forgetting about the others who looked on. Her body tensed as an overwhelming tingling sensation worked its way through her; her vision blurred; she felt lightheaded as her clitoris began pulsating.

He wasn't done. Gripping her hips, he pushed himself in deep. He rolled his hips in a circular motion, as he lifted her up slightly. With more room between them, he pulled out further, and his thrusts were longer; in deep he went, flexing his shaft as he pulled out. She began to tingle more. He pumped. He pushed. He circled out and then in. He thrust in hard, then pulling out slow. She could feel him swell even bigger, deep inside her. Her head began to spin; pulsating, her body began to shake; her whole body tightened as she felt herself partially blacking out; a sudden gushing deep within. All her energy was gone. She gripped him, holding him for just a moment.

Her head still spinning, she grabbed his lower jaw, and gave him the only kiss he would get. Leaving him tied at the neck, she buttoned up her long overcoat, shoving her clothes in her briefcase. She teased her hair, and straightened her coat. As the doors opened at Queen's Park, she looked at the men who now looked exhausted. "Gentleman!" She smiled, and stepped off....

Saddle Up

Katie was a little bit whiskey, and all country. There was no question that she was all woman, squeezed into her jeans. Her button up, long sleeve, flannel shirt, open down to just below her rib line; low cut white tank top, with her breasts pushing against the fabric. A man had to be careful not to look whenever she leaned over, or his eyes would be forever lost in the valley of the voluptuous hills. She was country specific from her Bullhide Pure Country Cowgirl Hat, to her brown and turquoise Marfa Leather Cowboy boots; and, her love for Ford Trucks – that misguided country love and diehard loyalty that she'll never get in return. A little bit of whiskey, a swath of Copenhagen, a country boy in tight jeans, and she was weak in the knees. While pursuing her equestrian studies at Mizzou, Missouri State University, she met her husband. He was tall and handsome, average build, but rugged all the same. They were deeply in love.

She was lost in thought prepping the Tennessee Walker, that stood before her, for therapy, when Sadie walked in. Katie's love of horses, lead her to where she was. After receiving her certification as an Equine Massage Therapist, she began working at a large breeding ranch just outside Columbia, Mo, while her husband continued with school. It was here that she established herself as a reputable therapist, and the ranch began to outsource her work. To help with the workload, the owner had begun to take on interns from Mizzou. The newest intern, Sadie, broke up the monotony of her life. Sadie was a young country woman, who liked to wear her camouflaged shirts open down the front, always showing off her assets. Sadie was definitely sexy, and as she watched her, Katie found herself attracted to her. They became close friends relatively quick; and, over the weeks Katie had talked to her about turning down the volume on her appearance, even if it was just making her display a little more country. Something about taking sexy to the country level makes everything acceptable, she told her. Not only was Sadie a beautiful woman, she was a beautiful person. She made everyone feel welcome. She made everyone feel wanted. The way Sadie looked at her, made her feel beautiful. The way Sadie touched her, made her feel desired. There was a moment, just the day before, that she felt herself lost in Sadie's touch; like she was outside of her body, watching as she leaned forward to kiss Sadie's lips. It was as if the fullness of those lips were pulling her in. She caught herself, not because she didn't want to kiss her, but she felt her insecurities creeping in – and didn't know how she would react. Sadie just stood before her smiling, her pearly white teeth gleaming from between those bright red lips. Her eyelids softened; her green eyes sparkling as she gazed into Katie's eyes. Katie felt her nerves taking control of her; She couldn't move; Her body feeling light, as Sadie tucked Katie's hair behind her ear. She caressed the ear as she withdrew her hand. She had never found herself so attracted to another female, but in Sadie, there was something special. There was something that just drew you in; something that made you want to hold her and not let her go; something that just made you drop what you were doing, just so there were no distractions while you were with her; something that just made you tingle deep within, when she looked deep into your eyes.

Katie's mind wandered back to when she and her husband toyed with the idea of being with another woman. Neither dedicated enough time to making that adventure happen; nor could she find a woman that she was attracted to enough to lay down with. It was a fleeting interest, but had Sadie been there it would have been more than fantasy. She wanted it for her husband. She wanted it for herself, to feel the touch of a woman. She wanted that feeling of opening herself up to a world of ecstasy, of passion, to one who knew how to please a woman - where most men fail to deliver. Every day that she saw Sadie, she felt that tingle. She believed Sadie knew it too; in the way she looked at her; in the way that she talked to her; in the way she touched her. That sexual tension continued to build, in the slow way they talked to each other; in the way they laughed more; in the way they began to pause longer in their glances. On this day, she was getting the Tennessee Walker situated, when Sadie entered the barn. When she entered, even the horses took notice. Katie turned not to stare, but it was hard not to. Sadie had taken her advice, and found the fashion she was looking for. From her Snakeskin Cowboy boots, to her Peter Grimm Rowdy Cheetah Cowboy Hat, Sadie's message was loud and clear – she was Wild Country! Her faded jeans were tight, outlining the gentle curves of her legs. Her shirt definitely form fitting, a Wrangler Ladies Angele Long Sleeve Snap Shirt, with that fading color that seemed to blend all the way down to her boots. Sadie could see that she had captured Katie's full attention. Their touching was gentle and purposeful. Their conversation was light and playful. That playful nature continued even after Katie's husband arrived. He had planned on picking her up her early, to take her to dinner for their wedding anniversary. Now, he just sat on the bench, watching the two of them rub that horse down. He joked with them about the attention they gave to the horse. How lucky could one horse be? She could see his excitement, every time he touched Katie. She could see his heart beat, when she ran her fingers through Katie's hair telling him how beautiful his wife was. She watched him shift in his seat, when she placed her open hand low on Katie's hip.

Sadie smiled, "You have to take care to touch the body, where it needs to be touched the most. You have to be rough, yet gentle, when grinding that muscle, to help improve blood circulation, joint mobility, and most importantly release tension." His attention was on her, and she moved her lips with full purpose of accentuating the words she spoke. She placed her hands on Katie's hips. "You see," she said, "a horse is not that much different than a man or woman. You just have to find those areas that motivate it to do what you want. You have to massage it to relax it in the right order, to get the most from your stimulation. If I am going to work on the muscle groups that surround the hips, I'm going to run my hands across its Lateral Vastus." Sadie demonstrated by slowly running her hand down Katie's hip, to her upper thigh. She placed her head on Katie's shoulder, looking directly into his eyes, as she rubbed her hand up and down, fingers spread with a gripping massage in her movement. "Then, once I have that area stimulated, I'm going to slowly move into the horse's more vital muscles like the Iliacus. Sadie moved her hands up the hip, and forward into Katie's pelvic region, with the same massaging pressure as before. She lifted her head, first kissing Katie's ear, and then her neck. Katie just stood still, with her hands on the horse, unable to move. She was nervous, and too excited to know what to do. This was new. Her adrenaline was rushing through her body, her heart beating faster. Sadie whispered into her ear, "Don't move!" As she threw down clean horse blankets, spreading them across the floor, she looked to Katie's husband. "I'm for her alone." Placing her hands on Katie's hips, she turned her around to face her. She could see Katie's nervousness in her eyes, her open lips, her deep breathing. She removed Katie's hat, letting it fall to the ground. Katie's scalp tingled as Sadie ran her fingers across her scalp. Her heart jumped as Sadie's soft lips touched hers. Her mind went blank as she felt Sadie's tongue against hers. She felt Sadie's hands gently feel their way down the front of her body, one button at a time, tugging at the flannel. She could feel Sadie's hands unbuckling, then working her belt out of its loops. Sadie took Katie by the hands, guiding her down onto the blankets. Pushing her white tank top up, Sadie explored the soft part of her lower abdomen with her lips; then tickled Katie's sunken belly button, first circling its depth with her tongue, and then adding a bit of seductive suction. She pushed the flannel shirt to the side, and pushed the white tank up - raised up putting her lips to Katie's once again. Her tongue went deep. Her kiss was long and passionate, as she unfastened Katie's bra. Grasping both breasts, she took them in her hands massaging deep. As she took one breast into her mouth, she slid the other hand down the front of Katie's jeans; the zipper unfastening as it followed the path of the hand. When Sadie's hand reached its destination, she scooped her fingers down and upward, causing Katie's back to arch, and bringing her chest up. As her husband slid in alongside her, she watched as Sadie stood and slowly dropped her clothes to the floor – everything but her hat. Her body possessed perfection so few could obtain. So glorious in its form, men desired to be near her, and women desired to be her. Her long blonde hair hanging casually down one side of her face, her lips so desirable that you never wanted to stop kissing them, eyes so captivating that you never wanted them to look away. The gentle slope of her neck, down to her shoulders, called to you; teased your lips that so wanted to taste its soft skin. Her breasts firm, and pushing out; gently rounding into the center of her chest, forming that valley so desired by many. Her body firm, tone, and built to be desired.

With boots off, Sadie removed Katie's pants the rest of the way. As she ran her hands up the now bare legs, she began teasing Katie's inner thighs with her lips. With her husband tending to her upper body, and Sadie exploring her lower, Katie found herself in a state of excitement she had never felt before. Sadie caressing those inner thighs with her tongue, and lips, was placing her in a state between crazy and ecstasy. She then felt Sadie's firm grasp of her hips, pulling herself in as she began licking Katie's plump outer lips, caressing them, tickling them, teasing them. Katie felt her breath lightly on her clitoris, and just when she thought Sadie was going to place her lips on it, she pulled away. She did it again, and again. She would torture Katie to bring her where she wanted her. When she heard Katie moan just a little, as if crying in anguish, she moved in. Spreading the vulvas, Sadie continued to tease her victim; flipping her tongue in rapid fashion she pulled the protective hood back and brought Katie's Clitoris to full bloom. She moved her tongue from side to side, then flicking it again in rapid fashion. Careful not to over stimulate, she dropped its soft cover. As she began to suck on this pleasure nub, she inserted her fingers gently in and out, feeling Katie's throbbing as she reached orgasm. Sadie then ran her fingers gently up her inner wall, to find the spot she needed. She could feel its texture. She could feel its slightly different nature. She flicked her fingers inward, as if telling Katie to come hither. Again, she flicked her fingers, and then moved them from side to side. Katie was young, so Sadie would have to give her more attention to awaken what lay deep within, that deep erogenous zone men seldom find and some women never experience. Katie gripped her man's erect member hard, pulling it. Her chest was filling with excitement, anguish, fear, love, freedom, all at once! She couldn't explain it. While Sadie brought every part of her body awake like it had never been before; she pulled his tip into her mouth. He ran his member across her open mouth, till the fruit of his loins came to rest between her lips. She took one in, as he kneeled beside her, coddling it with her tongue; rolling it gently within her jaws; suckling it ever so slightly, so as not to apply too much pressure. Stroking his full length, she held the most precious symbol of man captive behind her teeth. Sadie left her wanting, as she straddled her hips over Katie's, grinding down to feel the pressure; grinding down to feel the pleasure. Their hips moved in conjunction with one another, unlike a man and woman – where the woman had to move to hit the mark he couldn't find. It wasn't that Sadie was unselfish and driven by the same desires as a man, she simply understood what Katie needed – and to watch Katie be pleasured gave her more pleasure than being pleasured herself. She moved her hips to compliment Katie's. She moved her hips to give Katie the most pleasure. Her one hand gently pushing on Katie's abdomen, she used the other to massage the area above her pleasure – to enlighten its senses; to awaken its pleasure; to bring it out of hibernation. She lowered down, taking Katie's breasts into her hands once again. Sucking the precious life they give, she cupped her breasts with her hands, and then captured those breasts in her mouth. Her nipples were so succulent. Her nipples were so wanting. Her nipples were so ready. She bit at them. She nibbled on them. She sucked on them. She pushed Katie's husband aside, and saddled Katie about the jaws giving Katie a taste of what she had long desired. Where Katie felt short in experience, she made up for in poetry of tongue. Her tongue was so evidently enjoying the taste. Her tongue was so evidently aroused by the task of giving pleasure. Her tongue was so naturally skilled at this art of love. Sadie turned her body, running her hands down Katie's body, till her mouth once again found its pleasure - its purpose. Katie's husband once again left out. He watched from the sidelines, throbbing from his anticipation, from his need. He watched as Sadie raised up, grinding her pelvis into his wife's jaws, while she looked him directly in the eyes making his torture that much worse. Sadie's head popping forward as she gasped for air. Katie was hitting the mark. She felt her body tighten. She felt her body weaken. Coming down from her saddled position, Sadie moved directly between Katie's legs once again. Her mouth cupping Katie's most pleasurable point, she expelled hot air to heighten the senses. She took her most vulnerable part between her lips, flicking it with her tongue, and then proceeding to suction blood into its plump veins. Inserting her fingers between Katie's lips, she found her target once again. That spot that had yet to be awakened. It was the elusive erogenous zone which held Katie's greatest pleasure. She flicked it to come hither. She massaged it in circular motion. She then flicked it to come hither again and again. The blood was answering the call; she could feel it slightly swell. Katie's back arched. Her breasts reaching, launching upwards by the strength of her shoulders pushing off he ground. Her body shook. Her body tensed. She cried out. She cried out like she had never before. Her whole body felt the impact of Sadie's call. She went numb, as her body felt like her energy gushed from her lower body. She collapsed back on the blankets, dizzy, and exhausted.

Sadie, slowly kissed Katie's shivering tummy, her rapidly quivering heart between her breasts, and rest her lips on Katie's. She opened her eyes, and without looking at Katie's husband. "Relish what you have in her! Enjoy her! She is a precious one!" Sadie then grabbed her clothes and left the two of them alone. "Happy Anniversary!"

In The Shadows

In the darkness, she could see the shadows move. She could feel their presence. It was not a figment of her imagination; not something from the movies; not something in a fantasy world. There was something that lurked in the shadows. There was something that followed her. There was something that watched her in the night. There was someone whose breath she felt on her neck as she slept. She could feel the warm air. She could feel their lips so close to her skin that it took her breath away; she dare not open her eyes. It was frightening, yet sensual. It made her body tense, and aroused, at the same time. The excitement of the unknown, occupied her days and nights – she could think of little else. It made her head spin, and her blood flow. It was unbearable.

When she was but a little girl, Vanessa stood with her father, just a short distance off the porch, peering into the night sky as he pointed out constellations in the star filled sky.

As she looked from one end of the field to the next trying to pick out the shapes, she saw faint movement in the distant graveyard. It lay just on the edge of her father's land, on a hill some distance from their house. Although it didn't belong to them, her father had always maintained it. There was very little, if any, traffic at the old yard; but, she had never seen anyone there at night. She said nothing, but thought of it often. A week or so had passed, and she had made a routine of being out there around the same time of night as the night she saw the movement – always in hopes of seeing it again, although it frightened her. When she did, she ran and got her father. She watched his old truck bounce down the gravel road, his lantern make its way through the gate, and walk the graveyard a few times before getting back in the truck. This happened more than once, before she was given the "Never Cry Wolf" lecture. From that point on, she kept it to herself. She would watch the movement, and could tell from the distant shadow against the background of the night sky, that it was human – and most likely a man. It would seem to come, and disappear, around the large tomb of Andrei Gheata.

When her father had gone up to cut the grass, and pull weeds, she was sure to join him. The tomb was large, but seemed enormous considering it was the only tomb in the yard. All other graves were marked with headstones that were aged, and deteriorating. All of them, dating from the early 1900's back to the faded dates of unknown times. Gheata's seemed to be one of the oldest of the frontier era graves – its dates faded long before the others. One night, she watched the shadow stop. She was sure he was facing her. She was frightened, even though there was so much distance between them. Stepping off the porch, she walked through the front yard, into the field, in the direction of the graveyard. The distant shadow was no longer there, though she looked for some time. As she turned to head back to the porch, she saw him standing next to a tree, not too far from her. He was tall, clothed in all black, with short slick backed hair. He just looked at her, but in the shadow, she could barely make out a smile across his face. Then, by simply moving behind the tree, he disappeared. She circled the tree, but he was nowhere to be found. That was the last time she saw him, though she often felt his presence. She looked for the shadows well into her late teens, till she left for college.

After her father passed away, she had hesitated moving back to the old house. As his health declined, she had spent most of her time there anyway, caring for him. The more time she spent there, the more she realized how much she missed the old country. The commute was too much. So, she gave up her apartment in the city, and moved back to town. She would have the summer off with school being out, hopefully enough time to get things figured out. She had spent years teaching troubled kids - focusing on other people's problems, to help her face her own, or avoid dealing with them all together. After her father passed later that summer, she took a leave of absence to face those head on. It was too much for her to take on at one time. She could always go on to other things, when things had settled. At her father's funeral, one of the ladies had recommended a doctor, who held an office in town, if she needed to talk with someone. During the week, he worked for various hospitals which he traveled to during the day, but he would see patients for a couple of hours each evening when he got home. She had driven by the old house in the center of town, but would tell herself it wasn't necessary and drive on. But, she hadn't expected the change in feelings with her father being gone. There were no more distractions. She was in the house alone, and her old feelings would find their way back in. Despite years of therapy, and medication, those childhood anxieties would begin to resurface. They weren't nightmares as much as they were feelings. She felt herself being watched at night. She felt herself being touched. She felt a presence. At that moment, she began questioning her decision to move back in, despite the facts. It only got worse. The moment she arrived home for the night, she closed all her blinds to keep anyone from looking in. In her sleep, she felt herself being watched. It didn't awaken her, but made her sleep restless. Then, after weeks of the occasional restless nights, she could feel the man sitting in a chair next to her bed, and feel his hand upon her leg. He only looked at her; only touched her; and only made his presence known for that fleeting moment before she woke. Her fear didn't fade with each passing night; each touch of her leg; each stroke of her thigh; each kiss of her lips. She was already on medication for depression and anxiety; after all those years of self-doubt, unanswered questions, and people making her feel crazy, she had to do something. The medicines no longer seemed to be working. Her imagination was running wild, and she was no longer able to control it.

    Perhaps it was the rain that was keeping her up, or the lightening crashing down that kept her nerves on edge, but she was restless. She wandered out onto the porch, watching the rain come down, and the occasional illumination of the sky from distant lightening. There was always something very soothing about the rain, very comforting about watching the sky lit up at night by the distant forces of energy, and yet frightening seeing the dark shadows it created. Such a conflict of emotion whenever it occurred; she wanted it; she loved it; but, she feared it. She looked over to the graveyard, but the flashes of lightening were too quick for her to focus on any one thing. Gripping her robe just below her neck, she looked down upon the puddle forming at the bottom of the steps. As she watched the rain drops splashing down, keeping the pool in a state of disruption, she gathered her thoughts; she had to stop herself from thinking too much. Without looking to the graveyard again, she turned retreating to the house, locking the door behind her. It seemed like hours that she would lay in bed, unable to sleep. Then she felt his presence. With her back to the window, she lay with her eyes closed, afraid to turn and look. In her mind she could see him sitting in the chair alongside the bed, with legs crossed. The shadow of his head appeared just above the high back, and his hands hanging comfortably off the arms of the chair. This outline of him showing each time the curtain showed its true white color, and lightening brought the shadows to the room. She couldn't look, nor did she need to. She could feel him. She could feel him as he sat there watching her. She could feel him place his foot to the ground, and lift himself up from the chair. A struggle took place within her, part of her telling her that it was all in her mind and the other part her natural urge telling her to run from the unknown danger. His contact with her progressively more involved at each touch. At first, she could feel him in her dreams. She would awaken after his touch, or his kiss, but always found herself alone. She would begin to see the shadows in the graveyard once again.

Knowing that he might come would keep her up late at night, though she kept her eyes closed not wanting to see what she feared, not wanting to find out if it was a dream. Each night, about a week passing in between, she felt him there, watching her, touching her, kissing her; but, he had never harmed her. That didn't keep her from fearing him; fearing his darkness; fearing his control over her. Her heart beat more rapid as adrenaline filled her body. That struggle within her, causing her body to jerk at his touch, her breathing to become faint and rapid feeling his breath upon her. She pushed her face into the pillow, as she felt the bed sink down pulling her body towards him. He laid his hand on her thigh, stroking gently with his thumb, placing her more at ease.

Then, slowly moving his hand up her body, he began to pull the sheet back; she released her grip. He grabbed her calf lightly, as his hand moved up her leg. Her body shifting more, so her stomach lay flat on the mattress, backside now fully exposed. She felt his lips touch the sensitive skin, in the dip behind the knee, then behind the other knee. His grip on both legs was firm as his hands moved up the back of her legs, stopping where the legs curved up to meet her hips. She felt the mattress dip as he straddled her legs. His hands moved up covering her buttocks, squeezing lightly as they went. Pushing up her silk lingerie top, he kissed her just above her waistline, in the valley of the lower back. His hands extended, with his fingers spread, he pressed down lightly, rubbing her deep beneath the skin, as his fingers moved up her back. She could feel the dampness of his probing tongue, and his soft pressing lips, move about her back, working their way up. Her nerves remained on edge as she felt his lips approach her neck. The feel of his lips on the one ear she left exposed, bringing her anxiety up; all her muscles tightening at once. She felt something stirring in her chest; his dark presence consuming her mind and body. The last thing she felt was his lips on her neck. When she woke, there was nothing. She hadn't seen his face. She hadn't felt his person, with her own fingers. There were no marks on her neck to indicate that he had bit her, but she did not believe he had anyway. There was nothing; nothing to confirm to her that it was anything but her imagination.

Parked on the street, across from the doctor's old house, she waited for some sign of life within. It was a very old two story, with the gothic looking large rod iron fencing surrounding the perimeter of the house. Obviously built with old European influence, circular corner widows in rooms that were shaped like towers, with pointy cone shaped roofs. One of those houses that immediately made you think there was a damsel in distress just waiting to be rescued inside. She liked that old style, but it held a level of creepy wonderment for her too. As darkness began to fall, she saw an inside lamp light up what was most likely the study, then the entryway lit up. She must have missed him coming home. She walked across the street, running her hand along the fence not counting the rails her fingers tapped – more of a distraction to herself if anything. Her hands palming his sign "Dr. Andrew Ice". Without pausing, she pushed the large arching gate open, and made her way to the door before she could change her mind. The maid, an unhappy looking, middle aged, overweight, woman dressed in a black maid gown and a cloth white hat, answered the door chime. The maid waved her in, asked her if she had an appointment, and then disappeared into the study.

When the double doors opened, a tall handsome man, wearing a dark suit, stood in the doorway. "Vanessa. Please come in!" She looked at this man and hesitated. Her first thought was, how she could possibly explain to this man what dreams, visions, nightmares, or fantasies that she was having. She would be too embarrassed. As if reading her mind, he stepped across the entry way, squatted down in front of where she was seated, and placed his hands on top of hers. "It'll be all right Vanessa. I'm just here to try to help." At first she felt a warmth come over her, a feeling of comfort, but then the feeling of darkness joined in. She was feeling it here too, like a cloud, so knew she had little choice. It would seem like more than an hour that she sat explaining her experiences and the subsequent reoccurring, relatively unexplained and unproved events - which she believed to have happened. He had sat patiently listening. For a moment, she looked at him, and felt uncomfortable; with his head rising just above the high back leather chair, his arms hanging comfortably off the arms of the chair, and his legs crossed. She listened intently as he explained the need for her stop the medication. "Vanessa, what you are doing is putting a temporary patch on whatever is affecting you. You first have to recognize the problem. Then, you have to let the problem work itself out so that you know how to deal with it. The easy fix, of course, is to simply hide the pain with a pain killer, and hope it goes away!" He leaned forward, placing his hands on hers, as she sat with them folded across her thighs. "I'm not saying this will be easy, Vanessa. I'm not saying that this will solve all of your problems. What I am saying is that if your blood is not clean, then you will never be able to see things clearly. It's up to you." He had beautiful, dark brown eyes, and she found it hard to concentrate on anything he was saying. But, she agreed to stop her medication. For weeks, these sessions would continue, as would the periodic encounters. "Be patient," he would say, "it takes time for all that medicine to be purged from your system. You will continue to see things, and feel things. You will continue to have symptoms of withdrawal from the lack of medication. But, Vanessa, you have to do this for you. Right now, you're not sure what is real, and what is not, and that is because of the medication."

Each night she found herself staring across the hay fields, hoping to catch a glimpse of those shadows that lie in wait. Hoping that by the light of the moon, she could see what everyone said did not exist. These nights were filled with waiting. Waiting to see if this would be the night he would come; lying in bed wondering if he would join her; wondering each night; fearing to fall asleep each night. He would come on occasion. She could feel his presence, but couldn't gather the nerve to look at him. Even with her eyes closed, he would cover her face. Never would he bite her, but that didn't keep her from anticipating it. He explored her body. He touched her. He kissed her. He ran his hands the length of her legs, the length of her body, and the length of her arms till they were clasping each other's hands. She felt his lips inch their way across her body, around every curve from her ankles to her ears, and across her frame from one hip to the next. His tongue made its own written journal, her skin its canvas; a cursive art of undecipherable letters. But each morning, she would have nothing to convince herself that it was anything but a dream. There was nothing to dispel her fears; the darkness that surrounded him keeping her fears alive. Sometimes fearing that he was real, and sometimes fearing that he was not. Her dizzy spells reminding her that it may be the medication fading. As the weeks passed, he seemed to visit less and less. Her sessions at the doctor's office would seem more realistic than the possibility that her evening visitor was real. She could still feel his presence, but she felt the same dark feeling at the counselor's office. At times she would wait outside his office for so long before seeing him that she would have to wear a liner in her panties; she was dripping with so much anticipation of being taken. That dark powerful feeling stirred a sensation of arousal; a sensation of fear; a sensation of excitement, inside of her every time. It had to be that it was on her mind, that she was here to discuss those very feelings – there could be no other explanation. She would begin to find herself torn in her feelings between two men; the man who they would say does not exist, and the man who was there to help her find truth. They both made her nervous, yet they both were able to put her at ease; the doctor with his words, and her midnight visitor with his lips. The doctor held such power over her, as he sat comfortably in his chair, with his legs crossed like he was so relaxed. She found herself daydreaming during their sessions. His questions going unanswered, as she watched his hand lift to stroke his mouth and chin; oh, how she wished she were that hand. He was so kind, and mysterious. He was so gentle and soothing in his tone. Her initial attraction to him grew the more they spoke. Why was her life so screwed up? As her visits in the night had all but stopped, and her sessions with the doctor had continued, she found herself falling in love with a person, not the dream. She just had to conquer that need for the dream, and the power it had over her. One seemed just as strong as the other.

One evening, she could feel the anxiety creeping through her body, as clouds moved across the sky shielding the moon here and there. It brought that eerie, uncomfortable combination of light and shadows. On this night, the wind howled, the shadows beckoned, and the moon seemed such a powerful force. She stood in the doorway, the light from the kitchen giving her bathrobe a sheer look. When she was getting out of the shower, something tugged at her deep within. The wind whispered to her, as the tree limbs brushed across the bathroom window. Still wet, she made her way to the front door. The house seemed empty; feeling more alone than before. But, it wasn't really alone that she felt, there was something different. It was the house that felt empty; it was a feeling of being abandoned, knowing no one else believed what she was feeling. It was the feeling of being watched, but not knowing whose eyes were watching. It was the feeling of being touched, but turning to find no one there. It was the feeling of someone breathing on your neck, but unable to find where that warm air came from. It was that feeling that nothing was in your control, and your nerves are on edge in anticipation. One of those moments when you feel desperation, and the need to cry out for help, but unable to explain what for. She began to feel herself going backwards in time, as if she were starting her struggle all over again. In the blink of an eye, she was digressing. It had to be the medicine wearing off. This experience felt new.

Off in the distance, she saw a dark shadow move across the western field. His long stride gave lift to his cape, trailing along behind; floating; waving; sharply whipping the air into submission. He seemed to glide across the field with little effort. Then he was gone. The light faded, as scattered clouds moved across the sky. The shadows from the clouds played tricks on her eyes, as she continued to scan the field. She was so focused, so caught up in her search, that she was startled by the movement to the east. He was closer. She had caught sight of him just as he disappeared behind a tree, his cape trailing along behind. Her nerves peaked as he disappeared, but did not come out the other side of the tree. She couldn't have missed it. She watched him go behind the tree. She had to know. Pulling her robe tight to feel more secure, she stepped from the porch, slowly moving towards that distant tree. The whole time afraid to take her eyes off of the tree, for fear she would miss him coming out from behind; but, so afraid that if she didn't look around something would get her. Her glances were quick, and jerky, keeping the tree in sight. As her heart beat faster, thumping harder, filling with blood, it felt like it was growing in size. Her chest felt tight. Her lungs seemed unable to draw in enough air. As she rounded the tree, her heart jumped; she jumped. There was nothing there. There was no one.

She didn't see it, but she heard it; the muffled sound of footsteps. A glimpse of the cape, perhaps she may have seen. A tree not too far from where she stood. She could feel his presence. The grass pulled at the bottom of her robe, loosening the draw string as she moved towards the tree. She could feel the cool wind across her naked body, as the robe filled with air. Her anxiety grew. Her fear grew. Her heart beat faster. She could feel his darkness pulling her in. She wanted him. She wanted his dark nature inside of her. Tugging at the remainder of the knot, she let her robe open to the will of the wind. Her curves highlighted by the light of the moon, and the shadows of the darkness. Her skin crawled with anticipation of his touch; his feel; his bite. She let her robe fall to the ground, as he stepped out from behind the tree. It was him! It couldn't be! She had to be dreaming. It had to be her imagination. He was so tall. He was so handsome. But, it was his dark nature that so deeply aroused her, and drew her in. Placing his hand around her neck, he gazed deep into her eyes. His fingers gently followed the curve of her neck down to her shoulder; then, back along her collar bone. The tip of his index finger journeyed just above the bone, in that little valley; feeling its depth; feeling its tenderness; making his way to the soft, and vulnerable, jugular notch. He circled that notch gently, and then ran the tips of his fingers down cupping her left breast. His left hand caressing her neck, sending nervous tingles down through the center of her body. Gripping the back of her neck, his other hand around her hip, he pulled her in. It was a sensation like no other, his lips on hers; all her fears; all her excitement; and all her anxiety, consuming her body at once. Uncontrollable tears began rolling down her cheeks. The kiss was soft, and lingering; his tongue deep and probing. All her senses were being awakened by him, as he kissed her. He caressed the back of her scalp, bringing his fingers together then spreading them out again, tugging lightly on her hair. His other hand mapping out a winding path from her buttocks to her shoulders, with the very tips of his fingers. Her hair standing on end; her skin aroused. He kissed her neck. Her carotid artery pumped with anticipation. Down to her knees he pushed her, her hands on his shiny black slacks; she could see his pants begin to bulge out in the light. She unzipped his trousers, and pulled him free. His uncircumcised member cloaked in skin. She could feel his soft skin slide on her tongue, as his state of arousal became clear. It wasn't long before he took her by the hair, and gently lowered her to the ground. He was there for her.

Throwing his clothes to the side, he leaned over her, kissing her one last time. He rose up, throwing his cape over her face, so she could no longer see. She was in complete darkness. Her body shook as she breathed in. She could feel his hands explore her body. His lips caressed her neck, as he moved down her body; taking a light bite at her clavicle; the shock, and tickle, causing her chest to fill with air. The tease of his touching, causing her body to quiver in anticipation of what he might do. Her body tensed as she felt his teeth graze her nipples. Not being able to see changed everything for her. It was painful and exciting. The gentle suction of his lips on her breast putting her back at ease, then the light nibble on her nipple, raising her fears once again. Again he put her at ease, sucking, and caressing her nipple with his lips and tongue; only to make her body jump with a quick pinching between his teeth. For a moment he would pause, watching her breathing become more rapid, then tend to her other breast with the same dance. Lightly biting on her hardened nipple, then softly caressing with his tongue to put her at ease; making her feel safe once again. Then clenching his teeth around the thicker skin of her nipple, tugging lightly, as her chest rose up to meet him. Again and again, he danced between the two, raising her anticipation, and then putting her at ease. Her tummy pulled in as his lips moved down, kissing, swirling, tickling with his tongue. Her nerves were a wreck, not knowing his next move; seeing only darkness; relying on all her other senses to know his movements. Her body still shaking each time she breathed in and out. Her body flinched at his every touch. She spread her legs, inviting him; wanting him. She felt his lips gently exploring around where she wanted him the most, denying her what she needed the most. Her breathing was rapid, lifting the cape slightly; almost confining and depriving her of air as she breathed in. The fabric almost choking her as her lungs pulled it in, each time she felt his teeth. Her thighs jumped as his lips touched them, caressing them, kissing them. Again she felt his lips tease her outer lips; gently grabbing them with his lips, then his teeth. His tongue went deep. Her back was arched. She feared the bite; wanting it; waiting for it. Depriving her again, he kissed her outer lips, and then gently took them between his teeth. She could feel the razor sharp edge rising out of them, but not breaking the tender skin. He bit at her inner thigh; she gasped for air. The joyful pain aroused such fear, such excitement. She could feel the weight of his body moving up; her heart beat faster waiting for his next move. His lips were once again caressing her nipples, then the gentle scraping with the teeth. Her nipples so hard, she could feel them almost erupt. She could feel him move between her legs, as his nibbles served to distract her attention. He filled her with his darkness, so thick and dominating. He spread her legs wider as he pushed himself in. Her breath forced out at each thrust. The deep, thick, penetration, overwhelming to her without seeing, not knowing, just feeling. She felt his sharp teeth bite her nipple, causing her to suck the fabric of the cape deep in her mouth. Her back arched, he thrust in deep again. As she breathed out, tears rolled down her face in fear, in anticipation, in excitement. He bit the other nipple, piercing the skin; striking the nerve that shot straight down to her clitoris, making her cum each time he bit down. She could feel him swell inside her. His darkness grew larger deep within her. She was peaking; she could feel herself about to explode. Her body tingled, and then went numb. As she felt him pulsating within her, she felt his teeth on her neck. She felt the darkness she so wanted, pulling at her every fiber. Then her body tensed, her back arched, and she felt the pleasure pulsating through her body.

When she woke, she found herself naked in her bed, all alone, her robe draped over the high backed chair. A sinking feeling filled her chest. She was disappointed, but more scared than anything. How could she have imagined so much? She did not remember going to bed. It rattled her to think she was losing her mind. As she stepped into the bathroom, she caught her reflection in the mirror. Two small scrapes angled across the left side of her neck. She ran her fingers the length of them; they had barely broken the skin. There was no pain or sensitivity to the touch. Covering the scrapes with her hand, she fought against the notion that her dream was real. It had to have been from her fingernails, while caught up in the passion of the dream. She found herself panicked, frantically trying to convince herself that this wasn't real. Half dressed in her pajamas, wearing two different kinds of shoes, she tossed her purse in her car. She fumbled with the ignition, but had no keys. Flipping her way through her purse, her keys were nowhere to be found. The contents of her purse finding its way onto the passenger seat, handful by handful. No keys. She grabbed her purse, and ran back to the house. The front door was locked. She reached into her empty purse again, for the keys she did not have. This was not happening, she told herself. The back door was locked as well. She returned to the front porch, only to find the door still locked. She sat down on the floor of the porch, lightly bumping the back of her head against the outside wall. As she watched the living room curtains blow in and out of the open window, she could almost laugh at herself. What a mess she was!

She sat parked across the street from the doctor's office most of the day, waiting for him to get there; yelling quietly at those that looked at her, because there was no way for her to be discreetly impatient. Her hands clenched upon the steering wheel, watching, and waiting. When she could take no more of sitting in her car, feeling it begin to close in on her, she decided to see if at least the maid was there. No one answered. She sat on the front steps, chin resting in her palm and fingernails flicking the edge of her teeth, her anxiety increasing. As darkness began to fall upon the town, the door behind her opened. The maid looked at her, "You can come in, but you're going to have to wait a little." She said in a disgruntled voice, then turned and walked away. Vanessa sat down on the bench in the foyer. The ornate woodwork of the old house always putting her at ease; its dark stained, high arch, door frames rising up from the white marble floor. Scattered furniture and book shelves made from Brazilian

Rosewood, matched with dark leather chairs and sofas. It was definitely masculine in its appeal, and made her feel secure and protected. Lost in her thoughts, she did not even hear him come in. The sight of his shiny dark colored slacks standing before her put her back in the field; back into his arms; back onto her knees. She just looked up at him, her mouth falling open just a bit but no words able to come out. He reached out his hand to her, "C'mon Vanessa, you look like you've had a trying day." She took his hand, and he led her into his study. She struggled at explaining what her dream was, and how she battled with herself in the morning after seeing the scratches on her neck. There was no way that she could tell him everything. It just wasn't going to happen. She just needed him to ease her mind. "Vanessa, you are not crazy. You are not losing your mind. You are not alone in this struggle. Give yourself another week, and that medication will be completely out of your system. Then you will see."

    She tried not to think about the days of the week, but of course she couldn't avoid it. There was not going to be a simple vanishing of her problems, as long as she sat around thinking about them all the time. They had all but gone away, till this last unforgettable dream. She could think of nothing else; wondering if they would disappear just like that. If they were going to disappear simply because she was no longer medicated, then they never would have appeared to begin with. She wasn't medicated as a child, nor was she prone to fantastic fictional stories. These things worried her; weighed on her heavily. Why her?

The evening of the seventh day following her doctor's visit, she began to feel more comfortable and relaxed. If she was going to see him, the timing would be about right between his earlier visits. If she didn't see him now, then her burden may be lifted. She stood on the porch, where she always stood, with her arm wrapped around the post at the top of the stairs. For hours she stood, felt no discomfort, and saw no movement. Hanging on a nail, just behind the front door, her father's lantern still hung. She remembered all the times she sent him chasing ghosts in the graveyard, and smiled. There was still fuel, sloshing around in its small tank, and by the second match she had it lit. Pulling her robe tight, she made her way down the steps of the front porch. She was going. She felt strong. She felt relaxed. She felt herself. In her stubborn state of confidence, she made the journey on foot across the fields, down the hill, and back up the long hill where the cemetery lay. She needed to do this. Pushing the old gates open, letting their hinges scream without apology. The cemetery was empty. There were no shadows to challenge who was in control. There was no more fear. She pushed on the entry to the sealed tomb of Andrei Gheata. The door did not budge, sealed a long time ago. The light of the lantern flickered as she turned and walked around the graveyard. Having checked everywhere else, she sat down on a large bench across from Gheata's tomb. She was relieved that it was all in her mind, but disappointed all the same. For over an hour she sat in the quiet company of buried secrets, and unfulfilled dreams. They were not alone, for there was a sky full of stars to keep them company.

That silence was suddenly broken by the loud grinding of stone. It startled her, making her jump, knocking the lantern to the ground. The only thing she could hear was her heart thumping loudly, and rapidly. She couldn't move, as she watched the door to Gheata's tomb open. There the doctor stood, tall, dark hair, beautiful brown eyes; the whites of those eyes flickering in the flame of her lazy lamp. There was no cape this time; he wore no shirt, only black shiny slacks. He stepped from the tomb. "I've been waiting for a very long time Vanessa!" Placing his right thumb to her lips, he grabbed the hair on the back of her head, lifting her up. Looking into her eyes, he ran his thumb across her lips preparing them for the touch of his. It was a long kiss, no rush, just lips. Their lips together as if it had been centuries in the waiting. They took a breath, and kissed again. His tongue found hers, and they touched like they could never be separated again. There is no description for how the two felt inside. There is no description for how connected their souls were when they kissed. It was indescribable. He pulled her robe open, finding her breasts wanting, and willing. He gripped them like he never wanted to let go. Her neck so sweet to his lips, his tongue left jealous. Pulling her hair, he guided her down onto the large bench where she had been seated. As before, he teased her by nibbling her clavicle, bringing her body to arch up just a bit. Then taking her breast into his mouth, he pulled as much of it in as he could. Releasing his suction on her breast, he bit her nipple lightly striking the nerve to her pleasure. After awakening it, he gave suction to the sensitive nerve. She breathed in deep, quick; the air would then escape, releasing in short bursts. Then he began the same dance with her other wanting, willing, breast. His hand moving between her legs, he found her open. Deep into her he pushed with one finger, then a second. She moaned as he pushed against her already swollen clitoris. The tips of his fingers finding their mark, he flicked and circled that spot, her path to orgasm. He continued his dance between her breasts; her nipples made to be sensitive. He nibbled at them. He suctioned the life from them. He tickled them, imprisoned them with his lips, and then bit lightly at the nerve on each one. As his fingers moved in and out of her pleasure, circling, flicking, his lips made their way down below her ribs. The soft skin of her stomach made his lips feel youthful once again. He first kissed her inner thighs, then biting at them. He first kissed her outer lips, then biting at them. He moved back to her thighs, caressing them with his lips, teasing them with his tongue. She pulled his head in deeper. Taking her Labia Majora between his lips, he sucked on them, toying with their sensitivity; he kissed them gently. He scraped his teeth across the skin of her outer lips, causing her to flinch and gasp for air. Taking the vulva in his mouth, he sucked in her soft skin till he felt her pelvis push against his jaw. His tongue continued to explore, going deep, and circling till he brought it back out taking the vulva into his mouth once again. He rose up, unbuckling his belt, and unzipping his trousers. She reached into his pants, pulling his uncircumcised member from deep in the fabric. She wasn't dreaming. In her mouth she felt the soft skin spread, the shaft grow in thickness, and the fullness of his size. The power of his darkness spreading her jaws, as she tried to take him all in. He pushed against the back of her throat, and then drew it out slowly. Again, she took it in, and slowly out. He pulled her head back, putting his lips to hers, his tongue to hers. With passion, his tongue went deep. He lowered her back down, moving his lips to her most desirable neck. He scraped it with his teeth, bringing a rise to her chest as she filled it with air. She wrapped her legs around, encouraging him in, then pulling him in. His darkness spread her outer lips, opening her legs even wider. Gently he pushed himself in, preparing her for more. He thrust. He pushed. Her chest rose up to meet his, as he went even deeper. She could feel the grooves of the muscles in his back, becoming more pronounced, the deeper he pushed. Her breast met his open mouth when he was deep, and at her nipple he bit. Again he pushed, again he thrust, and again her nipples rose to be bit. Again he pushed, again he thrust, and again her nipples rose to be bit. She could feel the edge of his teeth as he sucked long and hard on the breast he held captive. He arched his hips forward, pushing his member up and deep, rubbing the mark of her passion. Again, and again, he arched, he pushed deep. She could feel him swell. She could feel him grow larger. She could feel him harden even more. She could feel it that much more. Her breathing became heavier. The passion felt more intense. She gripped his back, pulling herself tight, skin on skin. The sensation of the tingling ran the course of her body. The sensation, the darkness filled her mind, her chest, pushing her groin to be overly sensitive. She wanted him. She needed him. As she felt his member throb, and pulsate within her, she felt the power of his darkness strengthen and grow. She could feel the change within him. Her body tensed. Their release was simultaneous. Then she felt his lips move to her neck. She breathed in deep, waiting. She breathed in deep, wanting, anticipating. She could feel the tears begin to form at the edge of her eyes, and a quivering in her chest. She felt his teeth take her where she wanted to be. He took her willingly. His teeth would find their mark.

They lay embraced by each other, wrapped in each others arms, and lost in each others kiss, till just before the sun would rise. Taking her into his arms, he lifted her from the bench, carrying her into the tomb that had occupied so much of her life.

The Pittsburgh Estate

Everything about her life simply cried out, screaming at its boring state of affairs. She was trapped in a world of uneventful surroundings; uneventful relationships; and an uneventful lifestyle. She could see the boredom over fifteen (15) years whittle away at her marriage; depleting every ounce of excitement; depriving her of the very blood she needed to get through her day. Perhaps she had waited too long to escape it. So many times she had thought of changing her mediocre life, but failed to act. What would she have if she did? Where could she possibly go? What difference would it make after so long a time with one man, at her age? When she finally did conjure up the courage, she was unable to overcome the insecurities that held her back, and change the course that defined her life. Her daily routine was anything but exciting. She was dangerously close to being stuck in a deeply seated, boring, and depressing life; and, nine cats away from being the neighborhood cat lady. She could not shake how downtrodden, and helpless, that made her feel.

While most people dread having to go into work, her work was her only source of excitement. It wasn't because her work was so gratifying, it wasn't. It wasn't because her work was so exciting that she couldn't wait for the work week to start, it wasn't. It was because her simple life had forced her to live quietly in a world of fantasy; to fulfill her desire to be different; to fulfill her desire to live more than she had allowed herself to live before. She wanted to break free of the cage she had put herself in. She wanted to be free from the inhibitions her upbringing had planted deep in her psyche, as to what was acceptable. She wanted to be done with regret. But, she lived with it even at the one place that inspired her fantasies. Her fantasy began early each morning, and ended without being fulfilled each evening – five days a week. He walked past her desk every morning, and she found it impossible not to watch him approach. It took everything she had to not look obvious as she undressed him with her eyes.

She could feel the lump in her throat grow, as he stood near her desk looking at the printouts she had ready for him each day. It didn't seem to matter whether he stood sideways, or faced her straight on; the bulge in his pants made her heart beat a little faster. She could feel the tension in her throat, as it began to tighten, and her breathing become shallow. He always seemed to wear pants that highlighted his assets, and she was always grateful for its presence.

He never did seem to pay that much attention to her, during the time she had worked for him. She could understand. Her clothes were anything but extravagant; they were anything but flattering; they were anything but revealing. It wasn't that she didn't try; it was just that she lacked the confidence in her own beauty. She lacked the security of knowing that men desired her. She failed to recognize that there was something deeply attractive, and desirable, about her. So, she dressed herself exactly the way she felt about herself deep down. He, on the other hand, was drop dead gorgeous! His masculinity was overpowering to her. She felt her nerves on edge whenever he was around. He could have asked her anything, and she would have obeyed. Instead, she watched each day, as other women, whom she thought to be more attractive, enjoy his company in a way she only dreamed of. It wasn't just his attention, or his companionship. It wasn't just a simple lunch date here and there. She could hear the pleasure coming from his office. She could feel the pain of it not being her.

In the world of Real Estate, there is no shortage of attractive, well dressed, men and women. They are selling themselves, to help sell the properties they need gone. He dressed his part, and it was evident that he took good care of the body in which he used to sell himself. His hair slicked back slightly, always with a Five O'clock Shadow, and his clothes form fitting. He just seemed to never be less than perfect to her. She wasn't his secretary, so none of the women that entered his office ever really paid any notice to her. He managed the properties within the REIT, Real Estate Investment Trust, and she managed much of the Foreclosures on the investments they financed for others– so he wanted her close by. Being that close to him each day was difficult enough, but being next to his office made that torture pleasurable and unbearable at the same time.

She would watch, every couple of days, a beautiful woman approach his office, only to disappear behind a closed door, for a period of time she thought no man could live up to. The shuffling within the office gave her notice of what she was about to hear. She could picture his office in her mind, and see them move about without actually seeing. His chair would creak indicating he had gotten up to close the door. Each time she found herself tempted to check to see if the door was locked, a deep desire to see him in action. The gentle whisper of the woman told her that he was unbuttoning the woman's blouse, and then sliding his hand down her body to unclasp her skirt. She could hear it. She could feel it on her own body. She could see the skirt fall to the ground. The woman's long blonde hair wrapped in his hand, as he pulls her down so that she is kneeling before him. She could see the woman in her mind, wrapping her long thin fingers around his member, and then taking him into her mouth. It made her so wet, to think of this other woman being in the position she herself so wanted to be in. She looked about the office, as she slid her hand down between her own legs. The slight crackling of the wood frame of the couch, indicating that he had moved the woman to a lying position. There was little to no motion, just slight moaning. His head must have come to rest between her legs. As she could hear the woman's moans become more pronounced; more rapid; less controlled; less concerned for who could hear them, she found her own fingers rubbing deeper, and deeper, in more forceful circles. She began to forget where she was for a moment, till the cabinet drawer closed behind her. She gasped. So close to orgasm herself, her body struggled with the racing of her heart from her thoughts, and the racing from being startled. "Are you okay?" Her associate asked.

"Yes! Of course! Why?" She asked rapidly, looking down at her desk, shuffling papers.

"It's just that you look flush!"

"I'm fine, just feeling under the weather. Thanks!" She continued shuffling papers into a folder. Scolding herself, as she tried to answer. How embarrassed she was.

The moans quieted for a moment. Then she could hear the sound of skin sliding on the leather of the couch. The motion answered with more than just moans, more like grunts. They were deep grunts, like you hear from someone who was trying not to scream out. It was an unsuccessful battle to keep the moans quiet. The motion, continued, and continued. She could see the woman with her eyes closed, and her head back, taking him in – it's what she would do. While he was pushing deep, she would have her hands gripping his perfect buttocks, trying to get him even deeper. Her breathing was getting rapid once again, but she kept her hands on her desk holding the papers that shook in her hand. Her focus elsewhere, she failed to realize that she didn't really look like she was studying the papers. Eventually, the woman would leave his office, more complete than when she entered; more satisfied than when she came; in a better mood than when she arrived. That's what Victoria wanted, every day she came into work. It tormented her, while at the same time giving her pleasure. To live with a fantasy that wouldn't judge her; that wouldn't disappoint her; that brought her pleasure the way she wanted it brought; that made her feel desired the way she wanted to be desired.

Day in and day out, she relived her fantasy through the walls of that office. Some days the torture was more than she could bear. It was as if he was taunting her.

"Victoria, Jennifer and I will be in a meeting. If that paperwork comes through, just hold onto it if you will. Keep it, till we are done, and I will meet with you. Okay?" He would look at her with his deep blue eyes, making it difficult for her to respond. Jennifer was tall, athletic, with long brown hair. She worked at the other end of the building, as a receptionist. She had no reason to be in a meeting with him. They likely ran into each other in the break room, and talked over coffee. He was such a ladies' man, so smooth in his pursuit – they couldn't resist.

Oh how she wanted to be her, if only for a minute. She watched as they entered his office; his hand sliding along her waist as the door began to close. Strangely, it repulsed her how easily he moved from one woman to the next, but it pulled at her desires to be one of them at the same time. His ability to draw women in, and ability to satisfy each and every one of them, could not come without some expertise in his technique to fulfill a woman's needs in every way.

Once that door closed, she could see his hand move from Jennifer's back to her hip. His other hand gently reached up, caressing her neck, as he slid his fingers along its delicate lines and up the back of her scalp. The tips of his fingers making her scalp tingle. He would slowly, gently, move her up against the wall. Victoria could hear them pressing their bodies against it. She could feel his hand moving its way up the woman's skirt, finding the warmth between her thighs. Victoria heard her breathe in deep really quick, her breath shuttering just a bit, then moan to let him know that was the spot. She would raise her long leg, wrapping it around him, to keep him from taking away the hand. It was moving in all the right directions; it was touching in all the right spots. She pulled at her blouse, tugging it free from her skirt, and then unbuttoning it as fast she could while her lips sought his. He took his hand back up behind her head, grabbing a handful of hair as he pushed her to her knees. She released his member from its cloth prison, and took it into her mouth. Victoria could taste it. She could hear the moans through the wall. She knew what she would do. She knew how it would feel.

Her chest filled with air as her heart pumped faster, harder, and deeper; pumping blood into areas where she didn't know she had veins. Her body tingled the more she thought of the woman's tongue caressing his erect member. It had to fill her mouth, she knew it. It had to taste like hard pleasure; she could feel it in her mouth as her tongue rolled along its ridges. He would pull Jennifer up by her hair, and back her up against his desk; the papers falling off to the side as he lifted her up onto it. Her legs separated without so much as a command, as he lowered to explore her beauty.

The woman, lowered onto her elbows as he licked her; as he kissed her swelling lips; as he probed her with his tongue. She gasped for air. Her deep breaths followed by shuttered releases of air. Her senses aroused. Her abdomen tingling. Her groin throbbing from the pleasure it wanted, and pain from too much. Her hips felt as if they were curling inward from the pressure. Her thighs tightened their grip on his face. She grabbed him by the hair, pulling him in. "Don't stop!" she cried out.

He parted her legs, pushing her back onto the desk, as he pushed himself deep inside her. She gasped, an uncontrollable high pitched scream escaping her throat, as he forced his size upon her. She grunted, with her teeth clenched from him pulling on her shoulders as he pushed in deep, arching his member upward. Her head flipped back, she cried out again. Victoria could control herself no more, she moved the stapler between her legs, lifted slightly, placing it between the lips of her pleasure. She moved about as she continued to listen to the sounds coming from the office. The office she so desperately wanted to be locked in. The rounded top of the stapler resting perfectly between her thighs, she moved forward and back along its shaft. She could feel the chill of the pleasure up her back, her neck hairs curling upward. She tried her damndest to not get carried away, or draw attention to herself as she moved her hips in a circular motion. Between the sounds from the office, and the stiff shaft that lay between her legs, she would have momentary lapses of composure. Her elbows resting on her desk, she tensed; she felt the jolts of pleasure; matched with the pain of her throbbing with nothing to meet its pressure.

She watched as Jennifer left his office, still adjusting her outfit. This was Victoria's weekly routine. This was her torment. This was what fueled her fantasies. She just lacked the necessary aggressive tools, or drive, to go after what she wanted. Instead, she lived vicariously through the beautiful women who passed by her desk, and through their moans.

The next week, she would not have the same routine she was accustomed to. He was gone most of the week dealing with investors. One of their organization's clients, whose investments they financed, had fallen into deep financial trouble. They were busy picking up the pieces, pushing voluntary foreclosure, to take over said properties in a more timely fashion. Her boss rushed through the office, coming back from a meeting/golfing event. "Victoria, can you get me the file on the 151 First Side Condominium. I think we have someone to take that over. I'll need you to meet me there, to give the customer assurance on the ease of the process, Okay? Thanks!" He tapped his hand on the desk, and proceeded to his office in his green plaid golfing shirt, and white pants not as tight as his normal pants.

Victoria hurried to gather the file, and entered his unlocked office closing the door behind her. As she stepped into the office, she explained to him that part of the paperwork was already down at processing. His answer coming through the open door of his office bathroom, she thought nothing of it. She rounded the corner, to find him throwing his golf pants on a hanger. His black jockey shorts tight against his skin, outlining his package; the curves of his family jewels; the broadness of his head even in its soft form. The cuff, of the short legs, gripped the rise and fall in his muscular legs; waist band tight against his abdominal muscles. She followed the ripples of his stomach up to his bare chest. The muscles in his chest pushed his nipples outward. She couldn't help but stare. Her heart skipped a beat, only for a moment, and she thought that beat made its way into her throat. She couldn't breathe. She couldn't think. She couldn't move. As he buttoned up his shirt, he stepped towards the bathroom door. "You can just ride with me, Victoria. It'll be easier." He turned back towards the sink.

She turned to leave, but kept telling herself to stay. This was her opportunity to throw her inhibitions aside. This is what she had dreamed of. He was already half undressed. She wanted him. She stopped at the door, telling herself to just lock the door and take her chance. She locked the door, but stood there holding the knob. When he stepped out to tell her to give him fifteen minutes, all her thoughts collided. She was confused. She didn't know where she was. She didn't know what she was doing. It was all brief, but seemed like forever. She tried turning the knob, but it wouldn't turn. She pulled on the door, but it wouldn't open. She pulled again and again. Her frustration matched her confusion. She felt his hand slide over hers on the knob, stopping her for the moment, from her game of tug-of-war. He whispered into her ear. "I believe the door is locked. Let me help you." His hand was gentle on her waste, sending her heart into overdrive. She couldn't think or see now. The walls were closing in on her. This couldn't really be happening. The weight of his hand came to rest, down in the lower center of her back. He took his hand from hers, and unlocked the door. "Try it now." She felt her breath walk away with him when he left. She stood, with the door open a crack, fighting with her insecurities. They would win, once again.

The meeting at the 151 First Side Condominiums went very well. But how could you go wrong with luxury accommodations, in downtown Pittsburgh, so close to the

City's most sought after attractions. As he finished escorting the client to the door, she looked out upon Monongahela River, from the patio of the Penthouse of the 18 Story building. The view made her feel alive. The extravagance of this unit left her speechless. Who could afford such a life? The elegance made her feel beautiful. She could only dream of such things. As she watched the swirls in the river work their way down the channel, she felt his hands on her shoulder. She tensed up. He pulled her hair aside, and whispered in her ear. "Relax, Victoria." As his lips moved down her neck, barely touching, she couldn't breathe. He pulled her head to the side slightly, giving him greater access. His other hand moving slowly around her waist, down the front of her slacks, till he moved between her legs, and took her fully in his hand. He pressed in slightly, applying just enough pressure to awaken her needs. Taking her earlobe between his teeth, he nibbled, then tugged with a light suction and gripping with his lips. Her lungs weren't deep enough to take in the breath that her body screamed for in its excitement. Her chest filled beyond capacity, pushing her breasts up towards the sky. He slid his hand under her chin, griping her jaw, taking control of her movements. His lips caressed her ear, his tongue moving to penetrate its gentle curves. Deep it tickled. Deep it probed.

She pulled her suit jacket open, pulling at the sleeves, as he moved his hand up her blouse. Her buttons popped through their openings as if they couldn't get free soon enough. Her nipples poked through her blouse. As she pulled the garments from her body, he tugged at her slacks, dropping them to the deck of the patio. They were there for everyone to see. She could feel the air blow across her breasts, her senses heightened by the risqué nature of it all. She felt his hand in her hair grip tightly, as his lips explored her shoulders. His other hand slid up the back of her leg and buttocks, then around between her thighs. Pressing up, she felt his fingers enter her slightly. It was hard for her to breathe. She gripped the railing tight, as he curled his fingers up inside her. His tongue and lips caressing her jaw line, just below the ear. Her heart racing, she felt light headed and out of control – like she was floating. She could feel his manhood pressed against her buttocks, as his fingers made their way in and out. She breathed deep, trying not to hyperventilate. Her lips, and face, tingling.

He turned her, just like she had imagined so many times, and pulled her by the hair down to her knees. She ran her hands up his pants legs, across the bulge in his pants, to his waistline. Immediately, she began to pull at his dress belt and zipper. His mound of muscle hidden behind that fabric called to her; screamed for her attention; pleaded for her favor. As she pulled down on the black jockey shorts she had so wanted to be part of earlier, his hardened manhood pushed at the fabric. She felt it touch her fingers as she pulled at his waistband. It took her breath away for the moment. This was beyond her dreams; more than she could have ever thought possible. In its magnificent persistence, it popped over the horizon of the fabric in her fingers, coming to rest along her cheek. She felt its warmth. She felt its strength. She felt its firm tight skin, and commanding nature pressing against her cheek, just below her eye. Lowering her head slightly, she felt its tip. There was something sensitive about that touch. Tilting her head upward, she caressed his shaft with her lips, moving down to the sack that held his precious batter. Her lips explored their sensitivity. Her tongue explored their size, while she stroked his girth with hands that seemed tiny while wrapped around it. He tightened his grip on her hair, pushing it deep into her throat. Its true size could be felt as it stretched her throat. Out he pulled, then shoving it back in repeatedly striking the back of her throat.

Pulling her up by the hair, he pushed her against the railing. She felt his tongue pressed against hers, felt his lips gripping hers, felt his member pushing against her stomach. Turning her around, he pushed her shoulders down slightly. The head of his member spread her thighs to penetrate. She felt the tight pressure from having been so long. He felt enormous; she thought for sure he would tear her open. She felt him pushing in, the tightness making him that much harder. Unable to keep from crying out when he pushed his way in, her grunt echoed through the air. He thrust deep from behind, slowly at first. Harder he pushed, again and again, opening her up to take him in fully. She felt her legs weaken, her knees beginning to buckle. She couldn't breathe.

Pulling out, he turned her around, putting her back against the sliding glass door. He lifted her up from behind the knees, taking her up into his arms, with her back firmly against the glass. In one swift push, he was back inside her. She cried out in pain; cried out in joy; cried out in passion. His thrusts were deep, his size enormous to her. She felt her body quiver and quake as she came, again and again. Wrapping her arms around his neck, she pulled him in tight, holding him close, as her orgasms shook her body to the core. She didn't want it to stop. Carrying her into the kitchen, he laid her on the counter, stretching her one last time before pulling out. She felt his tongue separate her lower lips. He covered her pleasure with his mouth, breathing hot air to arouse her needs once more. Massaging her gentle areas with his lips and tongue, her head began to spin. Once more he covered her with his mouth, arousing her senses with hot air. She cried out. Her lungs felt light and empty, as she gasped for more air. The air escaping once again in a wave of breathes at each quiver of her loins. Her whole body was in erotic turmoil, feeling pleasure she had never felt before.

He lifted up from his task, his chest muscles filled and heaving in and out, as he prepared to punish her once again. She felt his strength spread her wide, and enter deep. Her whole body shook as he pumped, and pushed himself in deep. She had lost count of how many times she had reached her peak. She couldn't feel her lips, or her face. In the darkness of her ecstasy, she didn't even know if her eyes were open or closed. She felt him at every thrust; every time he spread her more as his member grew in its girth. She could feel his readiness. He filled her so well, she felt every pulsating throb of his member, as he released. He came to rest upon her. She didn't want it to end. She wrapped her arms around him, keeping him from pulling out just yet. Stumbling about, she had trouble walking; trouble balancing; trouble getting dressed. As uncomfortable as it seemed, she just couldn't find words to express herself during the ride back to the office. He was nonchalant about the whole thing, making her feel a bit more comfortable. She wanted what he had to offer, not a relationship. She could now relive it every time another woman entered his office. She could now close the door and lock it behind her, without thinking twice. He gave her the confidence in her beauty; the confidence in her sexual appeal; the confidence to take control of her life, the confidence that she so desperately sought.

A Little Wine On Ice

There was something about the atmosphere at Cedar Lake Winery that just filled your blood with romance, tantalized your mind and body, and aroused every sensual part of your being. It was more of an upscale rustic fine dining winery, and secluded escape, than what her and her friends would normally meet at. They would set to meet every other weekend, or as often as the girls could get away. Two of her friends were happily married, and the third just kept her boyfriend on a leash. It made her sick to hear how happy they all were, but she knew deep down that they weren't as happy as she thought they looked. Too many times she had fallen for the dream. Perhaps she fell too easy, just so she could fall way too hard. Not counting her less serious relationships that simply ended with her having given all for nothing - there were her two marriages that ended in failure.

The first marriage she chalked up to being too young. They had a lot of similar interests, but primarily just what each other brought to the bedroom. When reality set in several years down the road, and their differences began to rear their ugly head through the traditional combining of responsibilities, they began to go their separate ways. At first, their separation began to show through their visible dissatisfaction, then with their time. It wasn't long before they grew so far apart that they couldn't even communicate on the same level. One end of the conversation was frustration, while the other end was simply dismissive of the other. When the frustration became too much, she agreed to the divorce. The second marriage was not to suffer the same lengthy decline. Their interaction was constant, and their connection in the bedroom would make Larry Flynt blush. So, the moment she found out that he had cheated on her, she simply packed her bags. There could be no excuse that she neglected her husband's needs. He was a piece of shit, and there was no Doggy Bag big enough to put him in. She was beginning to wonder if what she had been through was now just making her too picky, but she knew what she needed to be happy. As desperate as she felt at times for the touch of a man, she wasn't willing to settle. If only she could satisfy her needs without having to deal with all the drama that came with a relationship, or the baggage that came with having to nurture a man's ego. As much as she wanted a man, she was tired of all the work required in having one. She sat, listening to her friends, as the wine began to loosen their tongues, and the problems began to flow as smooth as the wine.

The weather couldn't be more perfect, and the lake any more beautiful. A slight breeze made its way in and around the scattered picnic tables, and the sun not bearing down enough to make you sweat. She was glad she had taken her friends up on the invitation, not always making it to the bi-weekly get-togethers. Since the divorce, she had taken on a second job. She now worked two part-time jobs, just to make ends meet but keep her schedule flexible enough to be there when her kids needed her the most. The jobs she had paid the bills. They didn't define her as a person; they simply were what she had to do. The Post Office provided her with the flexibility to work during the day while her kids were at school. But, to fill in the gaps when her Post Office schedule couldn't quite meet her financial needs, she had begun to supplement her income with finishing furniture. The employer was flexible enough to work around her other schedules, he just needed cheap labor. So, while her kids broadened their minds at school, she labored away to put food on the table. Grinding, sanding, and staining furniture till she could no longer recognize her hands at the end of the day.

It wasn't often that she was able to break free from her busy life, or take time for herself. The kids always took first priority in her life, but she was always in need to replenish. Her mind would wander, as all the talk about their men left her out of the conversation. The giggling of her friends became faint in her ear, as she scanned the various groups of people lounging in the grass and gathering on the patio. The band, taking the stage, began to pick, thump, and tune their instruments to prepare every wine connoisseur for the interruption they were about to receive. As they began to play, a few women here and there began swaying with the music and snapping their fingers. The men remained standing stiff and talking amongst each other. Waiters and waitresses weaved their way between the groups tending to their needs, keeping the glasses happily filled. Melanie was beginning to feel the music herself. The Missouri made Norton Wine making its way into her bloodstream, and between her legs. She knew the more she drank, the worse she was going to get. The few scattered single men, that she did see, aroused no interest in her. But she was feeling the pressure; the need for the release only a man could give her.

    She caught a hint of his cologne as he brushed past her. His lightly checkered black and grey pants, slightly baggy on purpose. The material was light, and soft, so form fitting when and where they touched the skin. Had they not been baggy by design, there would almost be no purpose to wear pants at all. His oversized white shirt working to hide what was cloaked underneath. She watched his pants pull tighter, wrapping the fabric closely around his buttocks, as he leaned over the table just off to her right. She found herself for that brief moment wanting to be that fabric. At the moment, it wasn't important to her what he looked like. Her interest was solely in the young, firm, and perfectly rounded buttocks that the fabric was hugging. She could feel herself staring at it, not really caring if anyone saw, while she was trying to picture him without the pants on. The pants tightened even more as he leaned further across the large round table, gathering up the dishes on the table to throw them in his grey dish tub. But he was definitely not what you thought of when you thought of a Bus "Boy". When he turned, pushing his long blonde hair back and tucking it behind his ear, she could see he was very much a man. He looked to be in his mid-twenties, tall, with his mixed blondish brown hair resting just above his shoulder in a messy don't care style. His eyes were a bright blue. His slender face giving his appearance that more rustic, chiseled, masculine strength. That strength, that just made her want for him to take her right then and there. She watched as he picked his tub up off the table, and began walking towards them. She could see the movement of his balls from side to side as he walked. They could make the pants as baggy as they want, but it wasn't going to really hide anything. The fabric was soft, and effortless in its movement with the body.

As his member pushed against the stiffer material in the button up fly of the pants, the fabric curled back around to grip the curve of his balls. She could feel the wine breaking down her inhibitions, and her heart beating a little faster. He leaned against the table, bringing his balls to rest on the table pushing them up, as he set the tub down on the table in front of her. She was tempted to squeeze them, just to do it. But, just as she thought to reach for them, he leaned across the table grabbing the trash. "Pardon me, ladies. Let me get this trash out of your way." His voice was mellow, and comforting. Melanie, looked up, watching his smile, and the movement of his lips, as he talked to her friends. She reached out, cupping her hand around the back of his leg where the curve of his cheeks met his thighs, and squeezed lightly.

"I like your pants! They are so soft." She said, smiling. It was evident in his expression that he was a little startled.

"Melanie!" All three of her friends exclaimed.

"What? It needed grabbing!" She said, with a wink and a smile to her friends. Looking up at the Bus Boy, smiling, she tugged at his pants. "I'm kidding. I just wanted to feel the fabric." A little bit of sarcastic tone evident in her voice.

He walked away smiling, but looking awkward as if he wasn't sure how to really respond to the aggressive nature of her approach. Her friends were gasping, and voicing their shock at what she did. It really was not that big of a deal, she told them. He had a nice ass, and she wanted her hands on it - so she did it. They laughed and giggled, now having a winery story to tell all their other friends. Although they all expressed shock, Melanie knew they secretly wished they had had enough gumption to do it themselves. She watched the Bus Boy make his way from table to table, leaning over again and again, retrieving items left behind from those people too caught up in their fun to throw their own trash away. She would catch him periodically looking her way, making momentary eye contact, and looking away with an awkward smile. Whenever he would pass by their table again, she would toss a napkin on the ground, and smile. He'd smile, but pick it up without saying a word. "Don't forget this one!" She said, tossing another just a bit closer. It was the wine talking more than anything. "Go on! Bend over and get it. You know you want to!" Making her uninterrupted stare obvious, as she looked over her glass, curving her lips in an exaggerated fashion as she took another sip. She could see his cheeks flush slightly at the advance. As he leaned over to pick up the napkin, she ran her fingers through his hair. "Hey sexy, while you're down there....." A short laugh escaped, and his smile grew. He picked up the napkin, looked around the table at the women looking at him, and turned walking away. Once again, her friends were expressing their shock at her boldness, as if she was embarrassing them.

    The Bus Boy made his way across the lawn, through the scattering of people, looking back once for a quick glance, before disappearing behind a sea of people. She caught one last glimpse of him entering into an old white building that the winery used as a kitchen. The rickety old screen door closing behind him, the wood frames slapping against each other. Several times she watched him come and go from the building, their eyes making periodic brief contact. She took one last sip, finishing off her glass of wine, and stood up. "Okay, I'm not having this!" She waved off her friends, who called after her. "I'll be right back."

As she approached the old white building, the Bus Boy glanced over as he was entering the old screen door. She caught the door just as it was closing, not letting it slam behind her. After her eyes adjusted to the darker room, she could see it was set up primarily as a cleanup and dish washing area. The adjoining room, somewhat of a hallway to the kitchen, lined with shelving along each side for the clean dishes and pots and pans to be stacked. The Bus Boy stood looking at her, still holding the full tub in his hands. Stepping across the room, she looked into the hallway, and shut the door separating the two rooms. "Can I help you?" He said, a little startled at her entry.

"You can! Just be quiet!" She stepped towards him, taking the tub out of his hands, and throwing it on the counter. Her fingers pressing against his lips to keep him quiet, she pushed him back against the stainless steel counter. Her other hand, pressed against his chest, making its way down his abdomen to his groin. She took his bulge into her hand, and gripped him firmly, but not too rough. Taking a hold of his jaw, she put her lips to his; biting his lower lip as she squeezed him a little more. Kissing his chin, she ran her fingers tips across the back of his scalp. Lightly touching his Adam's apple with the tip of her tongue, she felt its hard bone-like structure between her lips. As she made her way up along his neck towards his ear, she tickled him with her lips. She whispered into his ear, "You know you want it, so don't make me hurt you!" Dropping down, she pulled at the buttons holding the soft material together at the fly. She could feel him begin to grow. Tugging at the fly to make the opening wider, she reached in pulling his briefs down, taking his member into her hand. The shaft filled quickly with his anticipation. Wrapping her lips around the head, she tickled its tip with her tongue, feeling it broaden. She cupped his balls in her hand, taking him fully into her mouth. Her jaws widening as the girth of his head pressed her tongue down. She could feel the stiff ridges of his shaft; the blood pumping through the enlarged muscle; her tongue running the length of his swollen veins. She stroked, and pulled at its strength. The feel of his solid erection, and his thickness pushing against the back of her throat, made the desire throbbing between her legs unbearable.

She stood up, pushing him aside. "Oh my god, just stick it in!" Reaching up under her skirt, she pulled her panties down, leaning over the stainless-steel counter. His grip on her hips took her breath away, as she waited so impatiently to feel the push deep inside her. She looked out through the dark screen of the door as people walked by. But, she could care less what anyone saw, as she felt him push himself past her vaginal lips. She could feel the pressure, making her so wet. Again and again, he pushed; he thrust; he moved; he spread. She could feel it up into her chest, as the aggression of his youth took control of her. He pushed her down on the counter, pushing harder and faster. The cries escaping her mouth were uncontrollable. Grabbing her by the hair, he cupped his hand around her mouth to muffle her screams. Again and again, he pushed deeper and harder. The pots and pans on the counter falling into the sink, and the dishes on the wall beginning to rattle, he pushed. His grip getting tighter, pulling at her hair and gripping tighter around her mouth, he thrust himself upon her, letting his desire take full control. The lips of her vaginal area feeling numb from the rhythm, feeling inflamed with pleasure. She could feel the darkness of the passion taking her body to a different place, the sensation tingling through her body, working its way up into her throat as she fought to breathe.

    She could see customers through the dark dirty screen of the door, oblivious to the backroom passion, as they walked past. As the euphoric feel ran its course through her body, she experienced moments of blackout. He felt more aggressive, stronger, and thicker, as the girth of his head expanded even more, as he approached climax. He pushed harder. Her covered screams were drowned out by the rattling of pans. For just a moment, she blacked out and all her built up tension was released. She caught her breath, with her face pressed against the cool stainless steel, as he pumped slower and slower, and the pulsating release became less as he came inside her. When he released his grip upon her, she lay for a second not wanting to lose the feeling. The noises from the customers walking by, reminding her that she had friends to get back to. She pulled up her panties, flipping her skirt back down. The Bus Boy buttoning his pants back up, looking at her like he didn't know what to say. She pushed against his chest, to make room for her to get by, and slapped his buttocks as she walked past. "Thanks!" She smiled, the screen door slamming against the wood frame as it closed behind her.

When she returned to her friends, they asked her what she was smiling about. "Nothing," she told them, "just feeling a lot more relaxed. I guess the wine is kicking in!" She felt much less stressed, and a lot less burdened by her cares of what people thought. There was no question that she was a little shocked herself, as to what she just did. Apparently, she had finally reached a point in her life where she just didn't care anymore. It was so liberating. The needless worries of meeting others expectations, lifted from her shoulders on this one afternoon. She never felt so relaxed before; never felt so in control of her life; never felt so powerful. Even her friends took notice, commenting on her demeanor a couple of times. They giggled, and joked with her about the Bus Boy who kept looking at her as he walked by. She paid him no mind, just smiling at her friends. But, she admitted to herself that she did appreciate his attention. She began to watch him again, another bottle of wine emptied amongst the friends; making eye contact with him as he made his way around the tables. They prodded her to drop a napkin on the ground, the next time he walked by. Melanie smiled, "Oh ye of simple pleasures!"

She called the Bus Boy over, curling her index finger inward commanding him to come closer. As he stood alongside the table, her friends were all looking on and giggling. She turned in her seat to face him, reached up, sticking her finger into the button fly opening of his pants and pulled at the material. Her friends gasped, "Melanie!"

He looked as startled as they did. Looking at his crotch, she tugged at his pants harder. "Do you know where I can get some sausage to go with my cheese and crackers? I like a lot of sausage with my wine." He covered himself, laughing awkwardly as he walked away. Her friends breaking out in laughter, shocked.

A managerial looking woman stopped him before he could make it back to the kitchen. She appeared to be pleading with him, as she pointed towards a log cabin style building off behind the other buildings. The building looked to have been an old barn at one time, refurbished into a beautiful gathering and banquet area. A large deck extended out from the upper floor, creating a covered patio for the banquet area below. Tables were scattered everywhere, covered in white cloth, and the center piece adorned with red and white roses. There was a stage off on the southwest corner of the patio to allow for entertainment, but the group that gathered there at the moment opted to use recorded music. She could hear it from time to time, whenever the band on the main stage by the lake was in between songs. She watched him nod to the woman, and disappear into the kitchen. Just as Melanie reached for the screen door it swung open, almost catching her in the face. The Bus Boy looked rushed. "I'm sorry! I have to go get this room set for later. I've got to go. " He said in an apologetic tone, and moved to get around her. His legs were moving as fast as they could without running, as he carried the heavy tray of plates large and small. The weight from the tray added strain to his legs, tightening and emphasizing the muscular curve of his buttocks; every curve, every dip, and every crease, visible as the cloth of his pants pulled firm at each long stride.

Through the open door, she followed him in at a distance. But, she was close enough to catch a glimpse of him as he disappeared up the stairs. The room was dark, and just rustic enough to stir the romantic in anyone whom entered. A casual seating area lay to the right, with the stone fireplace bringing an air of farmhouse comfort to perfect the setting. There seemed to be no one milling about on the main floor, the catering area to the left was prepped and ready for the guests on the patio when it came time for them to eat, and then the closed unmarked door for staff. Quietly, she made her way up the stairs, peering over the edge where the wall met the floor. She could see the bar straight ahead and the tall round topped tables here and there throughout the room. On the opposite wall a large television lay hidden behind wooden panels designed to match the wall, with double doors on each side leading out to the large deck. Enough light poured in through the large double doors that interior lights would kill the mood the room created. It was light enough to see, but dark enough to be erotic and sensual. She was reaching the top of the stairs, just as he made his way down the wall and behind the bar. As he bent over the cooler, she moved in behind him. He turned as her dress was dropping to the floor. "But!" He muttered, just before her lips closed over his.

"Shut up! Just get them pants off!" She grabbed him by the jaw, with her other hand gripping him by the hair. He grunted, startled by her biting his lip. His top buttons popping, as she pulled at his shirt. Kissing his chest, her teeth headed for his nipple. He let out a quick yelp of surprise from the pain. Moving his hands out of the way, she pulled at his pants to free them up the rest of the way. As she pushed them down, his excitement rose to meet her lips. His shaft pressed gently against her cheek. She opened her mouth, rubbing her lips along the edge before taking him into her hand. She stroked him, as she compared the size of his member to how small it made her hand seem. Circling her tongue around its head, she took him into her mouth. Moving her hand up and down his shaft, she could feel the ridges of its muscle. With her lips just below the curved edge of his head, she sucked hard to get it engaged. His eagerness became much clearer at each stroke of her hand, and hard erect nature making her wet. The feeling of having her mouth full from cheek to cheek brought her an unspeakable joy. That rock hard feeling rolling across her tongue. She took her time savoring the feel of the soft skin moving across the muscle, each time she worked her mouth up and down its shaft. The movement rattling the cooler he was against just a bit, she pushed open the sliding door that had slid open just a crack. Scooping up an ice cube, she placed it in her mouth. Getting her mouth chilled, she removed the cube and sucked on his nipples. A bit startled at the cold, he jumped. Placing the ice cube back into her mouth, down she went. The cold chill from her mouth caused the skin around his member to tighten, with his balls beginning to pull up and in. She heard him gasp, but not from the excitement. "Someone's coming!"

    She didn't have to look; she could hear the giggle from the couple coming from the deck. Lowering herself to the floor, she pulled him down on top of her. His chin resting on her ribs, just below her breasts. He looked to be nervous, and listening intently as the couple entered through the double door. "Shhh!" The young man whispered to the girl, as he closed the door behind them. Melanie slid further under the bar, to peak through the gap between the bottom of the bar and the floor. The couple began kissing, with the male pushing the female up against the wall. A passionate kiss, as his hands began to move all over the woman's body. Melanie looked at the Bus Boy and smiled, holding her finger up to her mouth to indicate he should be quiet. Taking the ice cube from her mouth, she rolled it around on her nipple, and winked at the man on her chest to finish the task. It was obvious that the Bus Boy was preoccupied with their predicament, and had lost some swollen interest. Turning her attention back to the young couple against the wall, she could hear that their panting had become heavier. Lifting her skirt, the man slid his hand between her legs gripping the woman's crotch to apply arousing pressure. Their breathing becoming louder, sounding like a mixture of moans and gasps for air. The woman dropped to her knees unzipping his trousers, and he gripped her by the hair shoving his penis in her mouth. Melanie watched the woman stroke him up and down, and try to take him deep into her throat again and again.

    Melanie could feel her own breathing becoming shallow, more rapid. She reached down, grabbing the Bus Boy by the hair, and pushed him down between her legs. When she didn't feel enough movement, she tightened her grip on his hair to get his tongue moving. She held him there, feeling his warm breath begin to tease her clitoris. He covered her pleasure with his mouth, blanketing her with hot air as he moved his tongue from side to side. Then, pulling his lips together, he kissed her gently up and down both sides before covering her vaginal area with his mouth. Again and again he repeated this circle watching her chest rise and fall with anticipation and arousal. Reaching up, he grabbed a clean dish cloth lying on the counter, and stuffed it into Melanie's mouth. Down he went, taking the hood of her clitoris between his lips, giving suction till he could feel the clitoris rise. As her pleasure began to swell, she bit down harder on the towel to keep from screaming. Gently, he slipped two fingers between her legs, spreading her vaginal lips, swiftly sliding them deep inside her. She tried to catch her breath with the towel still serving its purpose. With his fingers several inches deep, he could feel the soft circular patch of skin along her vaginal wall. He began to move his fingers in circular motion, awakening her G-Spot. As he moved to cover each breast with his mouth, he moved his fingers in a more rapid motion. The increased attention brought her to orgasm quickly. He slowed his motion, massaging the outside lips, and rubbing her clitoris gently till she would cum again. She could feel his fingers sliding back inside once again, sending a chill up her spine and her nostrils flared as she filled her lungs with air.

Feeling the sensations rising again, Melanie took the Bus Boy's hair tight within her grasp. The couple across the room lost in each other's touch. The man pulled her up by her hair, his erection standing between them. Pushing her against the wall, he appeared to be shoving his tongue as far down her throat as he could get it. The woman reached up, pulling the front of her dress down so that her breasts shot forward begging for attention. He met their request, devouring her nipples whole. As the woman cried out, Melanie felt her pleasure. When the woman gasped for air, Melanie felt her sensation. She watched the man place his hand under the woman's dress, and she could see in the woman's reaction when his fingers had entered her. As he hit the spot she needed touched the most, her back arched, pushing her breast against his lips. Not only could Melanie watch that pleasure, but she could feel the upward thrust of his fingers between her own legs. The Bus Boy continued his circle of pleasure, each time she reached orgasm he softened his approach and switched to bring her to orgasm again through other means. Melanie watched as the man grabbed the woman by the hair, spun her around, bending her over the tall chairs that circled the table next to them. Pushing her skirt up, he positioned his fully erect penis between her legs, and the woman's but cheeks shook just a bit as he pushed himself in. She gripped the chair, as he thrust repeatedly. With her breasts pressed against the seat, he pushed down on her neck as he aggressively rammed himself deep, pushing and pulling on her shoulders at the same time. The chair legs screamed as the metal sliders scraped the wood floor.

"Don't stop!" Melanie pulled the towel from her mouth, instructing the Bus Boy as she pushed his head down between her legs. She gripped the hand he was pleasuring her with, pulling at his wrist to keep his fingers deep within her. She could feel the woman's excitement, watching her eyes close and her mouth fall open the harder the man pushed. The woman lifting her ass end up slightly, pushing up on her toes, as she was reaching climax. She squealed, a muffled cry of jubilation. The man kept going, gripping her by the hair again, and pushing her to the ground. The thin round arch of her ass sticking high in the air, and her face pressed against the floor. He leaned over top of her pushing down, pushing in, and probing deep. The woman rolling her hips as he thrust in and out. Melanie watched as the woman approached climax again. With both hands on the woman's shoulders, he gripped her, and pulled on her body as he slammed himself in again and again. Finally he slowed, continuing to pump, not ready to pull out. Both of them were breathing heavy as he lowered himself down on top of her. Melanie came again and again, the Bus Boy hitting the right spots at the right moment. She felt her body quiver, a numbness roll through her body, and moments of the light around her fading. Her own body needing the break, she released her grip on the Bus Boy's hair, and just lay silent. She heard the couple rustling about to get dressed, and then shuffle out the door.

When the Bus Boy stood to make sure the couple had left, Melanie pushed on his legs backing him up against the cooler. Taking his softened member into her hands, she placed the head into her mouth and smiled as she gently held it between her teeth. She pushed his legs open slightly, and began kissing his inner thighs. With her tongue she mapped out a path from above his knee to the ticklish part of his thigh between his testicles and anus. Again she ran the length of his inner thigh, watching as he became aroused. Taking one of his balls into her mouth, and then the other, she gently rolled them on her tongue. As she stroked life back into his member, she ran her tongue up along its shaft. Cradling it in her hand, she pressed her lips and tongue against it giving suction to feel the skin tighten as it grew. Taking him into her mouth, she stroked and pushed his member deep into her throat; in and out; up and down she went. Running her hands up his abdomen, she gripped the muscles of his chest digging her nails in. He cried out in surprise. Melanie stood, with gritted teeth, and grabbed him by the hair. "You just need to FUCK ME!" She yanked his head back with a sharp tug of his hair.

The Bus Boy grabbed her by the hair, throwing her down over the cooler, her breasts landing in the compartment full of ice. She cried out. Slapping her hard across her ass, he shoved himself in between her legs, and gripped her by the throat as he pushed himself in. He ran his hand up the length of her back, digging the tips of his fingers into the muscles of her back, and then shoved his fingers into her mouth, gripping the bottom of her jaw. Melanie's teeth digging into his fingers as she bit down slightly, making his pounding that much more aggressive. The cooler rattled as he beat her thighs against the side of the cooler with his, shifting the ice around as it moved with the back and forth of her breasts. Another hard slap on her ass quieting her moans for the moment, gritting her teeth. He rubbed to ease her pain just a bit, only to slap her hard across the ass once again. It rattled her erogenous zone, and she could not hold back the yelp. "FUCK ME! JUST FUCK ME HARDER!" He grabbed a hand towel lying on the shelf, shoving it in her mouth. Her cries were muffled, as he slammed himself into her as hard as he could, pushing her further down into the ice. The cubes of ice numbed her nipples, and the cold chill on the skin surrounding them, beginning to bring her erotic pain. The yank of her hair, the slapping of her ass, and the bite from the cold ice against her bare skin, numbed all her other senses. She could feel the pain. She could feel the pleasure. The two combined amplifying her ecstasy. A stinging sensation splintered across her outer skin, making the euphoric numbness that rolled through her body that much more sensational. It felt, to her, like she was no longer in her body; no more than an observer, but able to feel and see the energy rushing through the body. She could feel him swelling inside her, his head expanding and its bottom ridge rubbing deep into her G-Spot. He continued slamming her against the cooler, rocking it off its legs at each forward thrust, back against the wall. She blacked out just as he was exploding deep inside her. The throbbing pulse of his shaft, pushed against her vaginal walls. Continuing to pump, he filled her with his semen, and then came to rest down upon her with his member still feeling her soft warmth inside.

After several minutes, when that erotic feeling had begun to fade, she pushed up. "Okay. Get up." She threw her dress back on, running her fingers through her hair. She grabbed him by the jaws, giving him a long kiss on the lips. "Phew! Thanks again!" With him still standing naked behind the bar, she made her way down the stairs. As she sat back down with her friends, they asked her where she had been.

Estelle, the friend to her immediate left, placed her hand on the top of Melanie's breast. "You're all red and freezing cold! What happened to you?"

"Nothing!" Melanie smiled. "My wine needed to be chilled! I'm good now!"

By The Light Of The Moon

With each stroke of her brush, she struggled to relieve the pain. There was so much of her marriage that was wonderful and memorable; but, right now, it simply felt like so much of her life was wasted. It felt as though she had lost so much time, so much opportunity to be happy. She felt as if she had sacrificed everything. The truth was that there was nothing lost; there was no time wasted. She had learned so much from it that she was stronger as a result; she was bolder than she had ever been before; she was a different woman.

She had chosen this apartment flat for its isolation, and the large picture windows throughout; the open aired look that the windows offered to the room and the relief from the walls that always seemed to be closing in on her. She thought that the openness would give her room to breathe; room to be creative; room to change. Her creativity was hindered by the claustrophobic feelings in her chest, and in her head. Even outside she would feel as if the walls were closing in. But, those same windows, at night, stirred her worst fears. The sudden change in emotion it stirred was hard, even if it was for the better. To uproot your life, lose everything you had spent years building with another person, only to start all over. All she had was her paintings, where she could lose herself in the canvass. The apartment offered her the room she needed to focus on her art; the space she needed to make her creativity flow; and an escape from her toxic marriage.

This was Johanna's new reality. To escape a relationship that endangered her ability to function as a woman. She needed the freedom to be herself, to give her creative spirit a little room to grow. The rent was low, as the district was still trying to be an up and coming area. It was an artist's dream home for inspiration. Although there were no retail or convenience stores contained within the blocks of old buildings, the main stream shopping districts weren't but a few minutes away. The city shadows, and the creatures that lurked within them, were pushed into the dark alleys that she could see the entrances of from her windows. This is where fear made itself at home. There was something alluring about the fear; about the anticipation that came with it; about the abrupt interruption it brought to her heart when her fears would make her jump at the littlest of things. There was an excitement hidden in those fears, something arousing to her; something dangerous and erotic. Each night she would stand in the darkness, when her mind was clouded with the images she wanted to paint. The images lingered on the edge of her fingertips, waiting to be released onto the canvass. The canvass waiting patiently as it rest on the stand, an arm's reach from her.

    The emptiness of her apartment flat seemed to echo off the downtown buildings, each and every time she looked out the large picture windows. She hated being alone more than anything. The shadows fueled her darkest nightmares, moving across the room in a nightly ballet with the city lights. At night, her paintings took on a darker image, reflecting her feelings. With her forehead pressed against the large glass, she would stare off down the vacated streets of the old warehouse district. She could see the river from her windows, just a glimpse; enough to catch the moonlight bouncing off the water between the old brick buildings. The streets were mostly vacant at night, even men often fearing to walk the streets. It's not that crime was as bad as the media made it out to be, it was the dark alleys; the unknown occupants of empty buildings; the absence of feeling secure between street lights; the use of streets such as this in too many scary films, now permanently labeled in the recesses of our mind as dangerous. She would see the occasional person walking hurriedly through the streets to get home, and the periodic drunk that would pass out in the street only for people to drive around him in the morning.

It was in the darkness that she was at her most vulnerable. It was then that she felt the most alone, the most betrayed; yet she also felt the most alive. The feeling of that chilled glass against her skin, made the night seem even darker. There was something about the chill in the night that made it quieter, mysterious, that much more dangerous. The shadows seemed thicker, and the street lights dimmed. The moon shining bright in all its glory, blanketing the night in a pale light that seemed to always call to the mischievous nature in all of us.

Out of the darkness he stumbled, making her jump. So caught up in the shadows, his sudden appearance startled her awake, the coffee in her cup spilling over onto her fingers. Under the watchful street light above, she gripped her chest as she watched him place his hand against the brick wall to keep from falling. A sudden fear came over her, seeing someone who appeared in so much pain but out of her reach. She felt herself pulled in several directions all at once; feeling the desire to run down to the street to make sure he was all right; feeling the need to call emergency services, to get him help on the way; feeling mandated to do something. She found herself with her hand pressed against the glass yelling to the man. Almost as if he could hear her, he looked up. His eyes penetrating her so deep she felt it weaken her knees. It took her breath away. There was something controlling about his gaze, taking possession of her inner core. She couldn't move. He straightened up, and his hand fumbled in the pocket of his long trench coat till it produced the keys to the door of the warehouse. He disappeared into the dark building, letting the man door close behind him.

For weeks Johanna watched the building across from her apartment hoping to catch a glimpse of him again. She hoped to see him during daylight to quash the anxiety that still stirred within her. There was something alluring about him; something that drew her in; something that held her attention captive. She couldn't think of anything but trying to narrow down his schedule, to make sure they ran into each other. His patterns were erratic throughout the day, nothing that she was able to pin down. He seemed to conduct most of his business by phone, focused more on his phone than where he was walking as he went to and from the building. In the evenings, on the other hand, she would catch a glimpse of him on occasion entering the warehouse. It frustrated her to the extent that she felt like going down and slapping him for not making it easier.

She stood at the window drinking her coffee, the one creature comfort she would not do without. It had become a ritual, for her creative process, making the special coffee. The long and tedious process of the French Press method gave her time to reflect on her thoughts, focus on her needs, plan her day, and evaluate her goals. It became more about the time it gave back to her than the bold rich flavor it offered to her passion for flavor. She stood at the counter, step by step she tended to the grounds that sat before her. Not grinding her beans too fine; finding that the pressing, and grinding by hand to be slow and methodic arousing the senses of needed pressure. The push, and grind, a symphony of pleasure; a fulfilling substitute for her inner most needs. The pressing of the grounds, a deep penetration she could feel within her bosom at each downward thrust. There was an erotic pleasure that flowed through her veins as her mouth waited in anticipation. She would often lose herself in the process.

Then she would sit and watch the evening news, glancing out the window from time to time. Another robbery here, another shooting there; the newswoman raising and lowering the pitch of her voice to add a little extra sensational drama to the story. Then she lowered her voice, to add deep concern, as she talked about another reported slaying in the park by what a witness believed to be a wolf. The drama only increased as another news anchor interrupted to imitate unplanned dramatic discussion, Johanna's attention faded as she stared into the streets below.

As he walked down the sidewalk, she caught him glimpsing up towards her window. She had had enough of this. In the kitchen, she pulled down the to-go cups and made herself one to go. She made her way across the street, and kicked the unmarked door several times to arouse the inhabitant within. When he opened the door, she took a deep breath, and handed him a cup of coffee. "You looked like a man who needs a good cup of coffee." It was obvious to her that she caught him off guard a bit, leaving him without words to respond – giving her a sense of power she so wanted. "I figured that I would bring my neighbor a cup of coffee, and find out what it was that you did here day and night. What odd business are you running across the street from my safe haven?" His eyes did not seem as piercing as they had before, but just as captivating. The ridge of his jaw line so sharp and pronounced; so firm and dominant; so strong and sensual, that she could feel the emotions stirring in her chest. His hair slicked back, trimmed neatly just above the neckline. He could take her at any time, she knew. A bit of control he didn't know he had, weakening any resistance she might have.

"Please, come in." Andre's voice was comforting, giving her chills up the back of her neck. The warehouse was dark, adding to the state of arousal she was feeling. Her nerves making her body feel lighter, and out of her control. She tried to breathe normal walking in through the dark corridor, fighting with that inner urge to let her clothes drop to the floor. She struggled to control herself, and not let this senseless collapse of her will be so obvious; reminding herself that they had just met. Perhaps she was lonelier than she thought; perhaps she had denied her needs more than she knew, and now it was all coming to the surface. Nature was taking over her body, and she couldn't think straight. Flipping her hair as he talked to her, not really hearing what he was saying. How silly she thought she must have looked, but she couldn't stop her body from giving off the signals to attract his attention. She found herself rocking from side to side as he talked about the artwork and artifacts he warehoused for prominent clients, acting as the middleman for high dollar deals. His clients were international, so his hours had to comply with the varying time zones. As fascinated as she was with the artwork that crowded the vast warehouse before her, it couldn't pull her attention from the movement of his lips; the reflection of light in his eyes; the shadows that highlighted the muscles of his jaw as he spoke.

He seemed somewhat distant, and reserve, in his interaction with her. She could feel that there might be an attraction on his part, but he was holding back. No matter how close she stood, or how obvious she made her interest to be, there was restraint in Andre's response. He wasn't married. According to everything that she did hear, she did not believe him to have a girlfriend, but she wasn't just going to come out and ask what his problem was. They had a common interest, and she was going to use that to get what she wanted. She had to know why he was holding back; it bothered her. Although she was soft spoken, and fragile, in many ways, when her determination kicked in she had unstoppable strength. For the next few days she pushed her way through his doors, with coffee in hand. She could see he was happy from the attention and company, though he remained slightly distant. He was reserve with her, but his eyes lit up when talking about the art that was placed in his care. He avoided answering too many personal questions, keeping his answers vague. Perhaps, she thought, he had a medical condition that kept him from wanting to let anyone in. That would give reason for his stumbling and disheveled look at night, a condition she had seen him in several times. He did not appear drunk, but she had yet to go down into the street and confront him. When asked, he simply blew it off as fatigue from working long hours. She would continue to pry, but get nowhere.

Each evening, she would find herself glancing to the street below her windows, ignoring her work that lay propped up before her needing completion. As she watched the shadows, she looked for him to come stumbling out from behind them. She was sure that she had just missed him in those moments that she had looked away. So, she leaned against the glass, each night, waiting. On this night, her heart jumped as he stumbled out of the dark shadows cloaking the street. Falling against the wall, he looked up, looking right into her eyes. It was that piercing look that she had seen once before; its dominance rippled through her body. She slipped on her shoes, grabbed her keys, and locked her door behind her. Her feet felt heavy on the stairs, not wanting to wait on the clunky old warehouse style elevator. The sole of her shoes catching the metal strips on the corners of the concrete stairs, making her hurried steps uncertain. The echo of her feet bouncing off the walls, making her heart beat faster, and her steps that much quicker. When she reached the bottom, she turned left to the door exiting into the alleyway. A sudden fear came upon her as she hit the darkness, not knowing what to expect. It wasn't that she had reason to fear, it was that she was so caught up in her rush to find out what he was doing, that she wasn't paying attention to her surroundings – causing her to fear what lurked in the dark corners she passed by, and now lay unexplored behind her. Too many late night attack stories on the news, perhaps; even though they were reported wolf or werewolf stories, which just seemed highly unlikely.

At the edge of the alley, where the building still blocked the light from the street, she stood. Waiting, with her shoulder feeling the uneven edges of the brick she leaned on, she wondered if she had missed him. She did not see where he had gone to, only assuming that he would have gone in his building. All that she could do is hope he was there, and to follow him when he left. It was crazy, she knew, but she just had to have an answer to ease her mind. The anticipation made her more aware of her nerves. The longer she waited the more calm she became. Her breathing slowed, as her heart slowed its pace.

In the far alley, down along the building where his art was stored, the door burst open. She could see the shadow stumble from the building, and her heart began to race again. He stumbled down the paved alley, falling against the wall twice along his way. As he moved further away from her, she ran across the street. She couldn't really see him, but she knew it was him. Peaking around the corner of the building, she could see him a short distance down the way. At a slow trot she made her way down the side of the building, trying to keep her shoes from making too much noise along the way, as she followed. The echo of the glass bottle she kicked made her heart jump into her throat, and she quickly took refuge behind the dumpster ahead. She could see him turning around, just as she ducked down. She waited. She could feel him looking down the alley behind him. Her heart was racing, with her breathing trying to keep pace. She waited. "What am I doing?" she asked herself, clinching her fists and closing her eyes. Every sound seemed louder, closer, and preying on her anxiety. The gap between the dumpster and the building offered her little view beyond the length of the wall. She could see shadows move on the wall, but little else. She waited.

If she waited too long she would lose sight of him completely. If he had suspected something, surely he would have walked back towards her by now. She waited. Extending her hand to grab the dumpster, she stopped herself. Again, she waited. It was getting the best of her. There was no more point in waiting. She grabbed a hold of the dumpster, pulling herself up and forward, to peek around the edge. There he stood. She jumped back. "What are you doing?" He asked.

"I don't know. I just wanted to see where it was that you go. It's like you're hiding something from me!" She defended.

"We are not together Johanna! You don't know me! " His eyes were piercing. His jaw was firm and clenched. He seemed different and definitely more aggressive to her. The muscles along his jaw line much more pronounced, and his skin tone seemed different. He grabbed her by the arm, gripping tightly. It frightened her. It was exhilarating. He led her, arm lifted up and pulling her forward, back down the alley towards her apartment at an aggressive pace. He released her as they neared the street. "Don't follow me! What I do is none of your business!" At that, he turned making his way back down the alley. He picked up the pace, not turning back, then broke into a run.

She stood for a moment startled at what had just transpired. In no time at all he was gone, fading into the darkness. Her heart still pumping from the rush of adrenaline, she was beside herself as to what to do. After staring into the black abyss at the end of the alley for some time, her shock wore off. She turned and headed back to her apartment. For the remainder of the night she stared at the blank canvass in front of her, the dark empty street and a taunting warehouse door visible out of the corner of her eye. Though she looked to her canvass waiting for inspiration, her mind was on that door waiting for it to show some sign of life behind it. That wish would go unanswered.

The next evening, with her lights turned out in her bedroom, she peered out the window waiting for him to make his way in. She watched as he slowly came into the light, looking up to her windows he would not find her there. But, his head turned slightly to the dark windows she hid behind. It was as if he could see her, for she thought they looked into each other's eyes. His eyes piercing through the glass, but she sensed there was pain behind them. When the door had closed securely behind him, she was off and running. She made her way out of the building, and down the alley she had been in the night before; a little panic set in as she passed the dumpster she had hid behind the time before. She looked back, relieved to find no one there. Hurriedly she moved to find cover beyond the alley before she could be seen. As she rounded the corner, she faintly heard that alley door open, as it bounced off the brick wall before swinging shut. Quickly, she ducked between two wholesale furniture store delivery trucks parked on the street, just outside their docking area. When Johanna saw Andre appear out from the alley, her heart stopped for a brief second. Taking in a deep breath, his nostrils flaring out, as he raised his head, he looked in her direction. She panicked.

He paused looking in her direction. Her heart racing; she could feel her blood pumping and her throat closing in. Then he turned, crossing the street, heading into the tree line that made up the perimeter of the St. Louis Arch grounds. She waited for a moment, then made her way across the street just outside of the reach of the street lights, and down along the wood line. As the cool air of the night had begun to settle in, by the light of the moon she could see the direction he had taken. His path was visible where his footsteps had disturbed the moisture in the grass; a darkened path where his weight had bent the damp grass down, showing his erratic pattern in and around trees. Slowly, she moved along the trees that lined the edge of the field, stopping every so often to scan the darkness and patches of the grey moonlit field for movement. The sound of tree branches cracking under the weight of the animals that traveled them, placing her nerves on edge. His trail continuing across the open field, in the direction of the river, towards the main body of the Arch grounds, she hurried across to the patch of trees midway across the field. Stopping in the trees, her heart beating so loud she could no longer hear the animals that lurked in the woods around. She leaned back against a tree, looking upon the open field ahead. His path was clear, towards the river bank he went.

Before she could move; before she could breathe; before his feet even hit the ground; she felt his hand around her throat. With his hand gripping tightly around her throat, he pushed her against the tree. "I told you not to follow me!" His tone was aggressive, and deeper than before. His eyes were fierce and penetrating. The overwhelming power she felt in his presence, rugged and dominating. Unshaven, and disheveled in his appearance, there was something unstable and frightening about him. She could feel his left hand gripping tighter around her throat, as he began to run his fingers through her hair. She couldn't move. With her heart rate accelerated, her breathing was unable to keep up. Blackness filled the edges, as tunnel vision set in. She could feel the sharp edges of his nails running along her scalp, around her ear, and down her neck. Thick, and long, they felt like more than just nails. These were not the well groomed nails of the man she talked about art with. This was nothing like she had felt before, during any of their previous contacts. The aggression that was so visible in his eyes, telling her that it was not safe to move.

She could feel his breath warming her skin, where her dress had failed to cover. His fingertips sliding down the side of her neck, and down along the neck line of her button up dress. The sharpness of his nails just lightly scratching the surface of the skin, as his fingers made their way down the curve of her cleavage. The tip of his nail coming to rest in the valley between her breasts, as her chest filled with the air of fear and anticipation. A top button, pulled tight in its pocket from the fullness of her breasts, kept his finger from going any further south. She closed her eyes as he moved closer. His face against hers, she could feel his breath along her cheek. With his lips gently tickling the edge of her ear, his deep voice rumbled in her ear. "You should not have followed me!" She felt the button pop, as he moved his finger down the front; the tip of his nail scraping the very edge of her skin on its way down. Her breathing becoming more rapid as each button gave way, till there were only a few buttons left to hold the dress around the legs. His hand now down between her thighs filling the gap between her legs, he pressed up and in. She could feel the sharpness of his teeth tease her neck and shoulders as he held her against the tree, and pushed his hand hard against her pleasure. She felt his strength, feeling weak against his power and control. He cut the bra strap in front, with one swipe of his hand, and gripped her breast, squeezing to push her nipple up and out. As his mouth consumed her breast, his teeth; teasing; tickling; and arousing pain around her nipple all at once.

He gripped her by the hair, releasing the pressure around her neck, and pushed her down to her knees, then face down holding her on the ground with his hand around the back of her neck. She could feel the fabric of her dress slide down her back as he pulled it towards him, tearing her panties away from her body. With one aggressive thrust, she felt his thickness forcing her open and her legs spread. Deep within her he pushed, placing his body on hers, she felt him gently bite her shoulder. The swelling of his shaft a stirring, hard, and needed pressure against her vaginal walls as he slowly pulled back, made her body feel alive. Gripping her by the shoulder and pulling back, pushing her head into the ground with his other hand, he slammed himself deep within her once again. The aggressive thrust pushing a muffled yelp from deep within her throat. Again and again, he thrust, as she took in a mouth full of grass. His size and aggression tearing her or making her extremely wet, she could not tell. The numb pain was not an unwanted pleasure. She gripped the ground, taking a hand full of soft dirt and grass, as he pushed again and again, driving her knees into the ground; spreading her wider; placing her thoughts in darkness. Her darkness littered with flashes of light, as he forced himself deep within, and her body shook each time he hit his mark. She felt her body go completely numb, and her body shook, as she came again and again. Lifting her up by the hair, he turned her upper body, and then flipped her leg over, leaving herself completely open and vulnerable to him. He gripped her breast, squeezing hard, and she felt his sharp teeth against her neck, as he pushed his hips forward.

His strength seemed to grow, and his girth seemed to expand. She could feel his body changing, and his passion becoming more aggressive. As she screamed out, he covered her mouth. Taking her nipple between his teeth, she could feel the edges of his teeth digging in as he sucked upon her breast. Her cries went unheard, silenced by the hand that imprisoned them. Her legs spread wide; she wrapped them around her captor. She lost herself at each thrust of his hips, all her worries escaping her. The growing muscles of his back stretched the fabric of his shirt. He was getting stronger. He was getting bigger. He was getting more aggressive. She dug her fingers in, as she felt him grow even larger inside her, pressing harder against her, moving faster and deeper within her. He scooped up her legs, just behind her knees, pushing her legs up towards her chest. Now he controlled her completely, gripping her about the neck, he slammed his hips against hers, and she cried out. Again, he pushed. Again, she felt him deep. Again, she felt his girth expand. From one end of her body to the next, she was shaking, quivering, and tingling. The orgasm assumed control of her body. She could feel his member pulsate, pushing at her vaginal walls, and tickling that most precious spot as he released. She gripped him, wrapping her arms and legs around his body holding him in. He lay on her for a second, and then tore himself loose from her grip. Without a word, he was gone.

For several minutes, she lay there not moving, covering herself with her dress loosely. Her body was still absorbing the euphoric rush of adrenaline, the indescribable numbness of pleasure. She made her way back to her flat, where she would sit in front of her canvass not painting anything.

The next evening she waited by the window, expecting him to come up to her flat, or acknowledge her as he went to his warehouse. He did neither. She didn't see him, so she either missed him or he never returned. But, the waiting just made her mad. The following evening, she waited down by the alley of her flat, and caught him just as he was entering the building. As he went to close his door, she stuck her foot in to stop it. She pushed the door open, poking him in the chest stepping him backwards into the entryway. "What was that?" She asked. "You throw me down in the park, and then don't even have the balls to contact me the next day. Now you're avoiding me?"

"I don't know what you are talking about. That wasn't me. I told you to stay away." He replied, looking uncomfortable. His response angered her even more. She couldn't believe he was trying to deny that it was him. The denial alone didn't confuse her, but the difference in his stature and his presence did. Why was it that he was a different person in the alley at night? Why was it that the man that stood before her didn't make her weak in the knees like the man in the field? She slapped him across the face, letting the door slam behind her. Not quite sure what she was angry about, whether it was his denial or that he was going to deprive her of what she thought she had found. Something pulled at her. The connection she felt may have been more driven by her loneliness, and the need for a man, but she had not expected that passion. She could feel him between her legs again. She could feel him pushing her to the ground. She could feel his teeth on her body. She felt a passion like she had never felt before. Her body was telling her that she craved it again, but her emotions were hurt by what appeared to be a rejection. That night she stewed in anger, at times crying.

By the next evening, she had regained her composure. She was angry, but not at the rejection. The fact was that she just wanted the passion. Men only seemed to hurt her, not lift her up. Andre obviously had issues, and secluded himself in his warehouse away from the rest of the world. But, that one night, by the light of the moon, in the middle of that field, he had become someone different. Another late night wolf attack story sensationalized in the news, toyed with her imagination. She flipped through her closet, finding her white Casual Cotton, Irregular Button High-Low Dress. With its sleeves down to the elbows, and its longer back side, it offered her the look of casual dress, while the front arched up around mid thigh drawing a man's eyes to its hidden bounty. She removed her bra and panties, allowing the hugging material to outline her curves. Down the stairs she went, across the street, and through the alley. She wasn't hiding her travels this time. Across the field to the patch of trees where he had taken her before, she waited.

The light from the moon coated the grass with a faint glow, and she could feel her anticipation growing. She wasn't afraid, but she could feel her nervousness grow. Not the nerves from fearing any rejection, but the nerves driven by anxiously waiting. He moved amongst the shadows of the far trees, she could see him as he stumbled and leaned against one tree after another. Then he appeared, moving quickly across the field towards the trees she stood behind. As he reached the edge of the tree line, she stepped out from behind the tree, standing before him. He was gritty, masculine, firm, and more aggressive looking as he had been their last night there. The moon outlined her body through the white cotton dress, her nipples poking hard at the material begging for attention. "Are you going to just deny being here now?" She grabbed his dress shirt just below the collar, ripping the buttons off as she pulled outward, and slapped him across the face.

He looked at her, his chest heaving. Grabbing her by the throat, he pushed her against the tree, shoving his thick fingers between her legs. "I told you to leave me be!" Moving his hand up inside her dress, he gripped her breast firmly, as he put his lips to hers. They were now both panting heavy. Down between her legs he moved his hand once again. Spreading her legs, he pushed two thick fingers up inside her. Gripping her neck, and shoving his fingers up deeper, he lifted her. With her back against the tree, she threw her legs over his shoulders to keep from falling. His jaw line tunneling between her thighs till his lips found their place. As he covered her pleasure with the warmth of his breath, and soft massaging movement of his tongue, her head tilted back against the tree and her eyes closed. He went deep with his tongue. It felt long in its pursuit and strong as it labored to move her body with its motion. She struggled to breathe at each flick of his tongue. When he moved it up one side and down the other, she felt the wave like a roll-a-coaster within her. He withdrew his tongue, cupping her with his mouth, heating her up with his breath. Slowly he massaged her outer lips with his lips, before sliding his tongue back in. Up and down again he moved her body with his tongue.

She released her grip on his hair, pulling her dress up over her head. The bark of the tree dug into her back. She grabbed his head once again, pulling him in till she could feel his jaw bone digging into her pelvis. She wanted him deeper. Her body shook as she came again, and again. He moved her with his tongue. He controlled her with its motion. Pushing against the tree, she pressed her hips up smashing his lips till she could feel herself grinding against his teeth. Up and down she motioned, pulling at the hair on his head, while her back knocked bark off the tree. She could feel no pain, only pleasure, but she screamed as though she were feeling both. Again she came, and her body shuttered as the orgasm rippled through her body. Sticking his hand between her legs, he lifted her up, catching her by the throat with the other, as he lowered her to the ground. He pulled at his trousers, releasing his throbbing member. With a quick yank of her hair, he pulled her head back slightly, placing it in her mouth. It seemed larger than most; its dark mass filling her mouth and pushing against her throat. She stroked the length of its shaft, feeling the veins and muscles hardening with life. He pulled her off, taking her to the ground.

She could feel him changing, his aggression growing. He gripped one breast, while he took the other one into his mouth. As he took her breast deep in his mouth, she could feel the edge of his teeth scraping her skin each time he gave suction. She gasped at the sharp pleasure of his teeth. The nibbling on her nipples sending conflicting signals through her body, a little pain mixed with pleasure. But, it was a pleasurable pain. As he bit lightly on her nipple, he slid his fingers between her legs, opening her up. Sliding one in, then another, he curled them up to find her G-spot, and he flicked his finger tips across it to test its continued sensitivity. She arched slightly, and he bit her breast as it pressed against his mouth. He then moved to her other breast, giving it its due attention, as he squeezed the free one firmly in his hand. Each time she arched her back with the flicking of his fingers, he bit at her breast, and squeezed. In smooth rapid motion, he rubbed his fingers back and forth, circling to change the rhythm, then back and forth again till she came. With her back arching, her eyes rolling back in her head, he could feel her body tense, then release. He pulled his fingers back, rubbing her clit in circular motion, then up and down, bringing her right back up to an orgasmic state. As she moved her pelvis back and forth keeping in time with his hand, he moved between her legs, and pushed his enlarged member between her lower lips. She gasped for air, feeling the sudden thrust, the sudden increase in size.

With his hardened shaft deep in her, he slid his arms under her legs, and grabbed her arms. She felt the sudden push against her vaginal walls as he lifted her up, his thickness making it known. He stood, pushing her back against the tree, spreading her legs out, he thrust upward. Deep within her he pushed, and lifting her upward as he pounded her pelvis with his. At each aggressive and probing thrust, her breath was forced out of her lungs. She could feel his muscles growing, his chest feeling as if it was covered with more hair. His grunting had become deeper and more animal like. Her body weak from the euphoric state he put her in, but he only seemed to get stronger. She could feel his nails digging in a little more. His pounding of her pleasure became more rapid, and dominating. He grabbed her by the hair, and stepped away from the tree. The only thing holding her up was his dick deep within her, hard, erect, and throbbing. Her legs dangled, as if she was suspended in the air. She felt its pressure.

He grabbed her leg, bending it, and turned her mid air. Grabbing her by the throat, he lowered her to the ground, and pushed down on her shoulders as he took her from behind. Her face in the grass, she attempted to catch her breath. Pounding against her, gripping her by the hips, he pushed in deeply and aggressively, as she cried her screams of pleasure into the dirt. He dug his nails along her backside and smacked her buttocks in a quick slashing motion, leaving a trail of scratches along its curves. Then, running his nails up her back, he dug his claws into her shoulders, pushing, pulling, pounding, and going deeper. His animal instincts taking control, there seemed to be no end to his mission to have her. The Werewolf within him taking full control, she lay there helpless, pressed hard against the ground, with the beast growing inside her. She could feel it. She didn't want it to end. Her body numb again, she could no longer tell if she was still hitting orgasm. All she knew is that she had never felt this light, this numb, this pain, this pleasure. When he released, when he came, he gripped her hips pulling her back and forth on his throbbing member. His panting and grunting more animal like than before. Then he was done. He pulled out, pushed her hips aside, and left her lying on the ground once again.

The White Knight

She was disillusioned by the dream. This dream that there was someone out there just for her. The dream that there was someone out there who was perfectly matched to handle the complicated person that she was so perceived to be. She wasn't at all. She was just an outspoken and honest woman, who came across as too sassy for most men to handle; a beautiful and intelligent woman, that just seemed to intimidate men.

Unable to understand what happened to men, and when they stopped being men; when they became overly sensitive; when they became emotionally unstable; when they didn't need someone to hold their hand. Where did the men go? She just couldn't catch a break. After another failed relationship, she was right back to questioning what was wrong with her. What was she doing wrong? Why couldn't she change? Why did she have to change? She just wanted to be happy. She just wanted to be swept off her feet. She just wanted a man who could handle her the way she was. At this point, she just seemed to be the ultimate matchmaker. Although she would never meet the person you were meant to spend the rest of your life with, you were sure to meet them while dating her – it just wouldn't be her! She thought her fiancé was the one. Three years they had been together. A week before their trip to Mexico, he ends it all without warning; to add more salt to the wound, her place next to him was immediately filled. Her friends were gracious enough to do what women do, to prolong her pain, sending her pictures of his social media posts while telling her how strong she is and what a dirt bag he was.

Attempting to escape her own pain, and loneliness, Kelsey took a friend up on her invitation to join them in Houston. The road down was long, lonely, and appeared uninhabitable at times. What a terrain this was, to make any kind of life. It was not just hot; it was a miserable dry heat. It was barren, not even the trees wanted to grow. The fields that surrounded her looked as unlovable as she felt. Who would want to live here? Who could love this misery? Who could love her?

On the side of the road, her emotions overwhelmed her. Sitting in scattered weeds up to her shoulders, her life seemed to be in free fall. It was already falling apart on her, now this. She should have seen it. She didn't need a cell phone to distract her while driving, her life was distracting enough! A crater sized pothole tore into her passenger side tires. The jolt sent all her belongings flying about her car; the contents of her purse strewn across the driver and passenger side floorboards. If she hadn't been holding onto the steering wheel at the time, she very well might have ended up in the ditch. After her car limped its way onto the shoulder, she looked at her car with disbelief. Even if she had the strength to pull her spare tire from the trunk, she would still need another tire. Not being near a town didn't help her, at all. She was a strong woman, but, at the moment, she lacked the strength to carry on. She just needed this moment in the weeds, to cry it out; while stranded in the pit of despair of some fairy tale ending gone bad. She wrapped her arms around her legs, burying her face in her knees, and the tears just flowed. She felt as desperate and abandoned as the ground she sat on. Her heart felt empty; her chest had a sinking feeling as if it was caving in where her heart had been; a painfully light feeling. She wanted it all out. She needed it all to stop. She needed for her world to stop spinning out of control.

As she sat wiping away the tears of stress, she heard the whinny of a horse not too far from where she sat. She saw the pointy ears begin to rise above the ridge line, the Stetson hat coming up not far behind. When he reached the top of the hill, his horse reared up on its hind legs; the rider, un-phased, holding the reigns.   Its front legs curled in, then kicking outward, coming down on all fours. Watching the horse dance around on the hill crest, Kelsey could suddenly hear Bonnie Tyler singing in her head; feel the beat pumping through her veins, and the words lifting her up. She needed a hero. She needed a knight on a fiery steed. She just needed someone to sweep her off of her feet, and make all her problems go away. Someone who makes her feel safe and secure, when she's at her most vulnerable. His horse never quite settled, just circling around popping his head forward to give warning of his aggressive obstinate nature. He was a beautiful grey American Quarter Horse; still young, so in transition and not fully white. The horse had such a unique and wild coloring mixture; a display of splashed grey and black patches, giving him a fierce and dominating appearance to match his personality. His muscles so pronounced, as he made his way down the bank of the dry creek. Kelsey watched the rider rock his upper body from side to side, balancing his weight with the movement of his horse. She could see his comfort in the saddle, his strength, his control, his domination of the powerful animal he sat upon. They disappeared from sight, down into the dried up creek.

She felt her heart, or maybe hope, jump up inside her, as she observed the horses head reappear at the gully's edge closer to her, and the white Stetson following along behind. The rider's shoulders were broad, his body trim, and strong. She could see it hidden under his plaid, long sleeve shirt. The collar of his shirt open at the top, flopping to the side, as it rocked with the climbing horse. Again, the horse reared up as it reached the top, its rider pulling the reigns to the side bringing him back down to a circling dance. She could feel his approach; every step the horse took towards her, a comforting and calming beat.

"Howdy ma'am!" Taking his fingers to the front rim of his hat, he tipped it slightly. "Looks like you are having a bad day." He cocked his head to the side slightly, with a slight smirk, as he looked at her car.

"You have no idea!" She almost choked on her words, trying to find her voice. Here her world was seemingly coming to an end, and this man comes trotting up; a strong, good looking cowboy, in the middle of nowhere. She was beginning to question how bad her luck actually was.

"I'm going to guess that you don't have anyone on the way." He said in a relaxing tone, and smiled.

"No." She shook her head.

"C'mon. You can ride back to the house with me. I'll come back and get your car. You're not going to get any help out here at this time of day, and it'll be too late by the time we get into town. We'll just get it back and see how bad off you are. Okeedoke?" He stepped down from his steed, and held out his hand to help her up.

She looked at the horse, whom she had watched shuffle around uncontrollably, throw its strength high into the air; and fight against giving control to his master. That made her nervous. The last thing she wanted to do was put her life in the hands of a large muscular animal, that didn't speak her language. In the past, whenever she had given control to a large, muscular, aggressive animal, at least they understood her commands – well, most men did; the others just spoke in sporadic grunts.

"Jack won't hurt you! He has a soft spot for pretty ladies!" His smooth deep voice and smile putting her concerns at ease. She took his hand, brushing the dust off her pants with the other. Looking into the cowboy's eyes, she ran her fingers through her hair tucking it behind her ear. It was a nervous reaction to his flirt, but also her natural feminine flirt to attract attention to herself. He cupped his hands, interlocking his fingers, giving her the original gentleman's hand-made lift to boost her up into the saddle. When Jack shuffled to the side, it frightened her. Brook placed his hand on her thigh, squeezing slightly, to keep her from jumping off the horse. His grip was firm, and drew her attention from the restless horse. "Hold on. I'm going to climb up behind you so you don't have to sit on the end of the saddle." He swung up, coming to rest behind her. His arms wrapped around her, holding the reigns. She found herself a little distracted from her problems by this cowboy seated behind her; pressed up against her; arms around her; with a saddle horn between her thighs. She felt him kick his heels against the steed as he clucked his tongue against the roof of his mouth, "Nht Nht!"

Back down into the gulley, and up the far bank they went. The ever expanding land ahead of them took her breath away. She would have a hard time finding Texas so bland after this. "My house is over yonder. Just bear with me, I just need to gather up a few of these calves and get them headed in the right direction." He pulled the reigns, leading Jack down the slope towards the river; a river that looked more like a small creek during the dry season. Only when the rains came, and the dry creeks were filled to their rims, did the river become a formidable destructive force. Standing in the relatively shallow river, a small calf stood still with the water up well past its legs. It seemed that each time the calf tried to move, it sunk a little deeper. Its cries began to echo in the little valley the high rivers had created. Brook turned Jack the horse sharply, and down the hill they went towards the screaming calf. Off the back of the horse Brook leaped, leaving Kelsey holding the reigns of a horse whose power she feared. Her legs tightened their grip on the saddle, and around the belly of Jack. She stiffened, pulling the reigns to her chest, afraid to move. The muscles of the horse, breaking the grip her feet had around its mid-section, not easing her panic of being on the beast alone. She watched as Brook made his way into the river to save the calf, but could only see him each time Jack circled back around. Her adrenaline pumped; her heart pounding; her racing blood fueling her anxiety. Then, when the chaos seemed to approach its peak, she found herself. Placing her hands on Jack's neck, she released the reigns. "Hey there!" She said, in her soft, comforting, feminine voice. Jack settled down, popping his head up a few times in defiance, before lowering his head in submission. Stroking his neck, and speaking calmly, she assured him.

Laying her head on his neck, she felt the sudden warmth in him; the warmth of submission; the warmth of trust that she had never felt in any male of any species. While gripping his neck, she looked upon Brook as he made his way into the river, to rescue the calf. She watched as the water line rose up on his tight fitting jeans at each forward movement of his legs. As the water crept up, and the faded coloring of the jean material turned dark, she found herself wondering what it felt like to be so wet, and tight, against his skin. The seam between his legs buckled up just below his crotch, putting a crease in the material. The crease, so deep in its inward grip, curved up between his legs and dominating bulge on both sides; creating a safety net of material, to hold and protect its cargo. She watched his swagger as he made his way up the bank, putting the calf to the ground. His shirt was soaked, and gripping to his body. The wet lower half of the shirt pulled at the material around his upper torso; its light grey, heavily worn fabric, hugging the curve of each muscle in his shoulders. His broad chest pushing at the material, making the shirt fit its every curve. Suddenly the saddle horn between her legs became a welcome accessory.

Brook walked towards the other cows, setting the calf down within view, and then slapped it across the behind to get it moving. He remained on foot so as not to get Kelsey wet. They weren't that far from the house, but it was long enough for her to realize what a genuine gentleman Brook was. He was laid back, with one of those comfortable demeanors that just put you at ease. The kind of demeanor that gave you the feeling he was just relaxed about everything, and always smiling. She opened up to him along the trail back to the house, how her luck had just seemed to abandon her and nothing would go right. He kind of smiled. "Well Kelsey, sometimes we wander off like a newborn calf. We unintentionally place ourselves down the wrong path, and find ourselves belly deep in water as we sink deeper in the river bed. It looked good at the time, and seemed like a really good idea, but then life has to send a cowboy along to put us back on the right path. It wasn't bad luck that sent him wandering into the arms of another woman; it was something telling you that you were headed down the wrong path." She nodded slightly, acknowledging his remark, but it was hard for her to actually feel the comfort from that line of thinking. She was sure he was right though.

When they arrived at the house, a quaint little ranch style house with a few scattered barns, Brook threw Jack's saddle and reigns up on the fence, and placed him in the corral beside the barn. After hooking up the trailer to his old beat up Chevy truck, he opened the passenger door, and waved her to get in. "Let's go get your bad luck off the side of the road." He smiled. There was just a simple down home feeling that began to set in as they rattled down the gravel road, in that old truck. It was a different kind of comfort. Not the comfort of a brand new car, and the luxurious feel it offered as you drove about town; but, that comfortable feeling at home feeling you get when the simplicity surrounding you makes you feel stress free. When the sound of an old truck rattling down the road, with country music playing across the radio, but barely loud enough to hear, is more fulfilling than riding in the back of a limo. Her car looked lonely along the side of the road, with the occasional car passing by. She stood by, watching her car hobble its way up the ramps onto the trailer. They weren't that far, so he didn't bother to strap it down.

At the house, he unloaded it from the trailer, and set it up on jacks. The rear tire first, and then the front. She felt helpless, standing there watching him working the tires off, rim and all, and then tossing them in the back of his truck. But, it was the "Uh Oh," that made her heart sink once again. "Well, Kelsey, it looks like your tie rod is broke. We'll pick one up in town while they're fixing you up some new tires." Before he could get to his feet, a large German Shepherd ran up excitedly, tongue and tail wagging, bumping him. He stood between the two, looking at Kelsey, while his tail continued to slap Brook across the face. "Kelsey, meet Kodiak. He's harmless, just been out rounding up the stray cows for me I guess. C'mon Kodiak, let's get washed up for dinner!"

Brook helped Kelsey carry her bag in, and set her up in the guest bedroom. The door didn't always latch, but it closed. He just hadn't gotten around to fixing it. If she had felt any reason to be concerned, she wouldn't have been staying the night to begin with. She threw her bag on the queen sized bed, admiring the simple furniture that occupied the room, and turned to make her way towards the rattling of pans in the kitchen. Leaning against the wall leading into the kitchen, she stood next to the refrigerator, and watched him as he pulled out all the things he needed to get dinner started. "Can I help?"

"Sure," he said. "I've got some potatoes here. If you want mashed potatoes, you can chop them up, or I'm just going to throw them on the grill. Otherwise, there's some mixings for a spinach salad you can throw together for me. The Red Wine Vinegar dressing recipe is right there next to the jar to shake it up in. While you're doing that, I'll get the grill going."

It may have been that he wasn't even trying to be romantic that made the whole situation so much more romantic and real, or just that she had never actually cooked a meal with a man in all of her relationships. They weren't tenderizing the meat as a team per say, but the fact that they were preparing the meal together hit a soft spot deep inside her - she could almost feel the tears well up in her eyes. It was one thing that she had wanted from a relationship was the companionship of cooking a simple meal together, or working in the yard together – neither of which did she ever think were overwhelming requests. Now she could feel it, but it wasn't really hers to possess. It didn't count, because she didn't even really know the guy. There had been a pressure in her chest which made her heart struggle to beat; a weight from all her anxiety, making her struggle to breathe at times, and making her forget to breathe the rest of the time. She could feel that weight, that heavy burden, begin to slowly lift.

It seemed so effortless; the most effortless time she had spent in a kitchen. The laughing and the joking, with the natural sarcastic and sexual banter that followed, that easy flow crept its way in as they prepared the dinner. A good bottle of Merlot to go with the steaks seared on the grill. It was refreshing from not only in seeing this type of partnership in a man's actions, but for her emotional well being - and exactly what she needed. They spent the remainder of the evening sitting out by the fire, with flames reaching upward toward the sky in the stone patio fire pit, laughing and talking. Kodiak sat next to her, with his head on her lap, soaking up the attention and the gentle stroke of her hand.

Later, when they had finally got around to cleaning up, they stood side by side at the sink; their arms rubbing against each other as they washed. She felt his hand on her hip, as he moved to reach around her grabbing another pot. His chest pressed against her shoulder. She stopped scrubbing for that moment, feeling his body against hers. That feeling of momentary pressure against her shoulder moved through her body downward, first stopping and hovering in her chest, then down between her legs. The thoughts in her head making her heart skip a beat, and her breathing shallow. "Press harder," she thought, wanting the weight of his body on hers. For that moment, pausing, and hoping she would feel his arms wrapping around her. But he unknowingly held his ground being as a gentleman, and they finished the dishes. They would sit and talk for a few hours more, with her taking every opportunity she could to show her willingness to flirt. She would bump him with her shoulder; lightly kick him with her foot as she laughed loudly at what he said, and touching his exposed arm. It was obvious he was a gentleman, but it was also obvious that he had been alone for way too long. He was missing the signs.

The next morning, Kelsey opened her eyes to find Kodiak with his head resting on the bed, ears up, watching her. He shuffled when she smiled, looking like he wanted to jump on the bed, licked his lips, and waited for her to move again. He looked so pretty with his black and brown face pressed down on the white sheets and his big brown eyes watching her every move. She could hear Brook pulling out pans in the kitchen. "Okay, okay. I'm up!" Kodiak jumped to his feet, with his tail wagging, as she threw back the sheets. She made her way into the kitchen, wearing just a t-shirt and pajama bottoms. "Good morning!" She stood looking at Brook, as he spread out his ingredients for breakfast.

"Good morning!" He turned, smiled, sliding her cup across the counter for coffee. "I need to run into town and get those tires, and a tie rod. Jim's shop will be open in about an hour. You are more than welcome to hang out here if you want. Parts get scarce at times out in the country, so hopefully he has a tie rod for your car in. How about a homemade Brook style breakfast wrap?"

"Sure. Can I help?" She walked over, placing her hand on his back. They talked and laughed at each other, as they went about cutting up the vegetables being thrown in with the eggs. She continued to bump him on occasion, flirting with him. It was the best breakfast wrap she had ever had, but perhaps it had more to do with who was making it.

After breakfast, they made their way into town. The tires were an easy replacement. The tie rod on the other hand, was not. Old Jim had used the last one he had in stock the previous week, and had just not gotten around to ordering any more. "I can have it here by late tomorrow at the earliest Brook." Jim placed the order for next day delivery, leaving her stuck for one more day. When it came down to it, she was not upset at all. During the extra time with Brook on the road back, she could see him loosening up. He had been very cordial and comfortable around her, but after breakfast and the trip to and from town, she began to feel him flirting back. That flirting continued when they got back that afternoon, helping him around the barn with chores, and then through the preparing of dinner.

That night, on the back patio, they sat around the fire drinking wine once again. When Kelsey finished her first small glass, she stood up to pour herself another. She then stepped over to Brook's chair, and topped off his glass. As she went to sit down alongside him, he moved his legs to give her room. She had changed clothes after dinner, putting on a clean white t-shirt, and sweat pants, with nothing underneath. With her back to the fire, the flickering light illuminated the form of her body underneath the shirt. He could see the curvature of her breasts, and her nipples begin to push through the fabric. She watched his eyes as they moved in glancing sweeps, trying to go without being noticed. Lifting her glass to her lips, she took another drink. Exaggerating the effort needed, she tilted her head back, and placed her hand on his thigh.

When she had swallowed the sip that required so much of her effort, she simply looked at him smiling with her hand still on his leg. The firelight still, and conveniently, highlighting the curve of her breast through her shirt. Brook reached up, sliding his fingers through her hair, cupping his hand around the back of her neck. He pulled her closer, his lips to hers. The fullness of their lips meeting as they gently pressed against each other. Pressing a little harder, they pushed forward to part ways, only to find each other again. This time, exploring each other's softness at length, they began to part to allow their tongues to meet in between. Tongues pressed against each other, another elongated sensual pause. Deep and sensual they went. It was more than a kiss; it was their bodies joining together as one. The harmony of movements an orchestrated symphony between their lips, tongues, and bodies pulling them closer. Without so much as a break in the passion building between them, Brook placed his glass to the ground, taking hers from her hand to do so as well. Their lips still engaged. He moved, his hand sliding it around her mid section, taking a hold along her back. With his tongue still keeping her distracted, he pulled her over his hips so that she came to rest on the reclined chair beside him.

His body pressed against hers, he could feel her leg begin to move along his. She began to moan lightly, as the kiss went deeper, and his hand tightened its grip on her body. His hand pushing against her ribs as he slid her shirt upward, her breasts now exposed. She squirmed, but did not resist, her legs moving, signaling the anxiety building between her legs. He took her breast into his mouth, gripping the other firmly. As he consumed her nipple, trying to pull its very life from it, he slid his hand down along her waist. Her legs kicking frantically to help slide her pants down and off. He grabbed her by the hips, flipping her over so that she lay face down. Slowly he outlined the curves in the small of her back with his tongue. His fingers made their way up her inner thigh, grabbing what he desired with one hand. Then, gently, he began to measure the distance between curves with his lips, in the valley of her lower back; making his way up to the base of her neck. He gave special attention to that lonely area between the shoulder blades, where the blades are not permitted to meet. That lonely, seductive, and alluring area tickled by the kisses of another. He moved to the ear she lent him, whispering nothing at all. Nothing said, nothing lost, but just enough so she could feel the words on the edge of her ear. That space between tickle and eroticism, where the word is so unimportant, but the thoughts it provokes placed her on that cloud not to be disturbed.

He ran his coarse, calloused, hand, across her soft supple skin. The contrast of the two in motion aroused her senses, as he moved his hand up the curve of her leg. Applying a firm, yet gentle, grip; a strong, yet soft, pressure on her thighs, he moved up her exposed, vulnerable, naked bodice. His lips sought to find her heartbeat, and count the beats of each chamber with his probing tongue. He ran his fingers through her long brown hair, caressing her scalp, then gently, but firmly tugged backward pulling her chin up, and then cradled her neck with his jowls like a vampire in heat. Kelsey forgot where she was. She felt his thick fingers slip between her legs, as his mouth returned to her breasts. She was already quite wet, so the two thick fingers that sought to probe her pleasure were in with no resistance at all. Her breathing changed the moment they pushed against her vaginal walls, her breast pressing against his face as she gripped the back of his head and his fingers went deep. His lips, and his pressing tongue, worked their way down her ribs, across her tummy, and down to her parting thighs. The softness of his lips between her legs, made her lower lips swell, her inner thighs pulsate with anticipation. As he caressed the soft skin, in the valley of her upper thigh, the curves disappeared as her legs spread wider. The thick fingers that kept her torture at bay, pushing deeper inside. His lips moving up her inner thigh, caressing her soft lips that gripped his fingers so tightly, and then taking her clitoris between his lips he aroused her every sense.

Giving her clitoris a little suction, manipulating its hood between his lips, he curled his fingers upward to find the mark of her passion. He tickled its fancy, bringing its sensitivity to life. She arched her back, pushing into him, his lips and tongue, his thick fingers, pressing him deeper into her vulva and labia capitulating grip. Surrendering to his lips, and his penetrating tongue, she opened herself up. The flipping of his fingers brought her to an excited state; her heartbeat rising; her breathing becoming heavier. She could feel the passion begin to roll through her body, the thumping of her heart becoming more pronounced. Her head feeling light, and her eyes rolling back into her head, she could feel the rush of the passion approach. Finding it difficult to take a breath as her muscle tightened, and her back arched upward. She released what air she had in her chest, as she sunk into the darkness, felt her blood rush through her body, and the gushing release between her legs. He moved his fingers from between her lips, and replaced them with his tongue. Flipping his tongue up and down, he spread her labia left and right with the pressing of his lips to give his tongue room to dive deeper in. He pulled back, covering her pleasure with his mouth, releasing the hot air from his lungs, to awaken her senses and arouse her desire for more. Again he parted her lips, pushing further in with his tongue. Her chest rising up, she grabbed the back of his head not wanting to let him out. He flipped his tongue up and down, maneuvered his jaws, his lips, his tongue side to side. Gripping her lips with his, then releasing. Taking her clitoris into his mouth, he pulled at it sucking in. She gasped. He lifted its hood, flipping his tongue at its most sensitive erection. Then down between her lips he went again; pushing; probing; massaging it with his tongue.

He rose up to take off his shirt, and Kelsey leaped up grabbing at his belt and pulling at his button fly jeans. Before he could get his shirt all the way off, she had his cock in her hand. She looked upon it for only a second, it was a beautiful thing. She paused watching it grow in width, the head enlarging, before she took him into her mouth. Its skin was soft and rolling, as she moved it with her tongue. He began to fill her mouth. Grabbing her by the hair, he held her on his shaft as he kicked his pants the rest of the way off. Lowering her down, their lips locked once again, as their tongues began a new dance. His fingers found their way between her legs, to keep her aroused and ready. Moving his legs between hers, she opened her legs wide to wrap around him. She could feel the difference in size between his fingers and the head of his cock. Pushing up and down slightly, he gently loosened her guarded pleasure to be forcefully spread. Moving his hips in a circular fashion, he slid himself in slowly at first. His enlarged head pushed at the sensitive skin of her pleasure, preparing her for what was to come. Thrusting forward hard, he spread her vulva and labia wide, her vaginal walls throbbed from the pressure against them, her chest sunk inward as the air escaped her lungs and a restrained scream escaped her throat. He was in, and he was in deep. Gripping his shoulders, she pulled herself up wrapping her arms around his neck. She could feel his muscles flex, hard, firm, and smooth under his skin, as he thrust forward again and again. He pushed the screams out from the depths of her diaphragm, resonating up through her throat, and pushing through her clenched teeth.

As the chair began to slide across the patio stones, from the forceful motion of the two bodies moving forward and aft, Kelsey began to slide off to one side. She was not about to let this little inconvenience bring an end to a moment she could have only wished for. She turned, placing her hands upon the ground. He grabbed her ankle as she moved her leg over between them. Kneeling on the chair, with her head now in the downward position closer to her hands, he grabbed her by the hips and pulled her in. The chair moved and rocked to the side as her knees dug into the BroyerK Outdoor Lounge Chair, dragging it with her across the patio. This modified Doggy Style position, pushing his member down, and across that sensitive patch where orgasms tend to hide. She could feel his hardened shaft, with its ribbed muscular swollen texture, moving forward and dragging back across the wall of her precious patch of skin. The pressure tingled her spine up to the base of her neck, as she began to reach orgasm. She dropped to her elbows, letting out a scream, as she felt a nervous energy ripple through her body. Her back arched as she came again and again, and felt moments of blacking out. The sweat rolled off her back in the dry heat of the Texas evening. They lay on the chair, side by side, when they were both spent. He handed her, her glass of wine, and they lay along their sides with his arm wrapped around her, catching their breath.

In the morning, she woke up in Brook's bed, with an overwhelmingly erotic warm and wet feeling growing between her legs. She had felt the moving of her legs in her dream, a movement that felt real, felt physical and stirring to her body's core. Brook's head lifted the sheet that lay covering her legs. That warm wet feeling was coming from between them. She felt his hands sliding up between her knees, parting her legs. His lips caressed the inner part of her thighs as they moved up, not far behind his hands. She could feel herself getting aroused as his fingertips pushed at her skin, and he kissed the sensitive inner thigh on one side, and then the other. She surrendered to him without a fight, opening her legs. It was a different sensation being awakened by sex. Not quite fully awake, but the sudden rush of her blood, and the increased flow of oxygen as her lungs filled with air, brought her to her senses quickly. He kissed her thighs, first with his lips, then with an open mouth pulling his lips in as he ran his tongue across her skin. She felt him breathing his hot air on her pleasure, as he teased her outer lips with his. First he kissed the soft skin, pushing at them with his lips, then kissing them with an open mouth; again moving his tongue across the skin as he pulled his lips together. He moved from one side to the other, giving each of her swelling lips the attention they needed, then back and forth again rubbing and teasing her clitoris with the tip of his nose as he did. He ran his tongue up the middle of her pleasure, flipping, moving side to side, then up to her clitoris. With his tongue, he first lifted the hood that protected it, and then spread it, moving side to side slightly as he closed his lips down on it. Like any good French kiss, she did not want this one to end. That warm feeling filled the lower region of her body, and a tingling sensation ran up her spine making her feel lightheaded.

He circled his tongue as he breathed warm air into the folds of her most precious of skin. She breathed deep, arching her lower back. He circled his tongue again, kissing her outer lips with his lips, then with his tongue as he manipulated her pleasure with his lips. Pulling back the hood of her clitoris, he flicked it with his tongue, then moved his tongue across it gently from side to side, before taking it between his lips and sucking on it cloaked in the hood. She gasped, grabbing the head under the sheet, and pushing down, forgetting a man lie beneath. His lips and jaws smashed between her legs, against her pleasure, she could feel his teeth pressed against her muscle, but she did not let go. His hair was caught in the sheet she gripped so tightly, and she pulled it as he slid his fingers between her lips and up along her vaginal wall. Pushing at her soft internal walls, he pressed upward feeling the rough skin. It was already awake and sensitive, and he felt her pulling down harder on the sheet as his scalp began to feel the pain. He moved his fingers in a circular motion, flicked them just a bit, and then circled, as he manipulated her clitoris between his lips.

As her legs began to move around showing their anxiousness and tighten, he pulled out, and began teasing her thighs with his lips. Running his fingers down to outline what he desired most, he spread the tips out to the crease where the pelvis and thighs met. He pushed down on the soft part of her butt cheeks sticking out, pulling her outer lips tight. He flicked her clitoris with his tongue, then began kissing her outer lips with an open mouth; breathing his warm air on them, lapping them with his tongue, manipulating them with his lips. Then, he put his fingers back in. As her hips tightened, and her back arched, he could feel her pressing down on his head. He took her clitoris back between his lips, applying a little pressure, then pulling at it with deep suction. With the repeated pressure, suction, and manipulation with the tongue, her chest began to feel light pushing upward as her abdominal muscles tensed up, and her legs tightened once again. He moved his fingers in a rapid circular motion, and then flicked them assertively against her inner wall. Harder and harder he gave suction to her pleasure, and faster and faster he flipped his fingers to her pleasure. He could feel her whole body tighten, her knuckles digging into the sheet that covered his head pushing down. He could feel her arching back, and her body shake, as her thighs clenched the sides of his face. He reached up under the sheet, and took her breast in his hand squeezing, pressing on her nipple. She cried out slightly as her breath escaped her lungs. Her body shuttered, and her eyes rolled back into her head as she came again. He kept pursing her pleasure, and she wouldn't release him anyway. With every flick of his tongue, and every flick of his finger, her head moved with them. She came again, barely escaping the first cloak of euphoric darkness before he was taking her there again, and again. Releasing her grip on his hair, and the sheet that held him down, she pulled the sheets in to her chest and just lay there for a moment with her eyes closed. Escaping the sheet, he leaned over her, kissing her on the lips. "Whenever you are ready, I almost have breakfast ready. I just need to throw the eggs on the grill. No rush, I'll bring you breakfast in bed." He smiled.

Kelsey gleamed, unable to control the wave of emotion it caused after all she had been through. He had gotten up early, and fixed her an omelet the way she had requested the morning before. She hid her face as he left the room. After all she had been through, that gesture and the way he woke her up on this morning, was simply overwhelming to her. She lay in bed, not wanting the scenery around her to change.

When she rolled out of bed, after pulling herself together, she made her way into the kitchen. He turned, with his spatula in hand, to find her still fully naked, and smiled. She walked straight to him, placing the palms of her hands on his broad chest, and looked him in the eyes, as she kissed him. A slow, full locking of lips with no movement between them, as her lips pressed against his. "I don't want to meet my friends." She said, looking deep into his eyes.

"Then don't." His jaw was firm, and his look was serious. She could feel he meant it. With the bacon sizzling in the background, she moved her hands down to his waist, and lowered to her knees as she unbuckled his jeans. As the bulge caught under his jeans grew, she pulled at the button fly front, and pulled down to set his manhood free. Taking him into his mouth, the head of his cock was large and smooth, with a pronounced ridge to tickle any woman's pleasure. He grew, filling her mouth, and pressing her tongue down with its stiffened shaft. "Kelsey, the eggs are burning!"

Taking her mouth off his member for only a second, "I'll eat them burnt!" she said, returning to the task at hand. Holding his enlarged shaft, stroking its hardened muscle, she took one of his balls into her mouth and sucked on it, then the other. She licked at the sensitive area just underneath the balls, feeling his legs move at the tickle. Taking him in once again, she moved down his member slowly, feeling every ridge and every vein with her tongue. She loved the rugged soft texture against her tongue. He threw the spatula on the counter, grabbing her under the arms, and lifted her up. Pushing her back against the center island, he placed his hand between her legs, and his lips to hers. His tongue went deep, and the passion in the kiss was just as penetrating. Turning her, by the grip of her hair, he moved her over to the main counter. With his hands under her armpits, he lifted her onto the counter, pushing her shoulders back against the cabinets as he pulled her hips forward. His member fully erect, with its skin tight and screaming, it poked at her thighs teasingly. She wrapped her legs around his waist, her heels pushing at his buttocks. As he spread her pleasure with the dominating passion of his member, her head banged against the cabinet door. He pushed in deep, grabbing her by the hips, he pulled her towards him. She cried out, hitting her head again. As he pulled out slowly, he slid his arms under her legs lifting them up, spreading her a little wider. He gripped her by the skin and fat of her buttocks, and pushed in, slamming his pelvis into hers. Again, and again, she cried out, as his shaft penetrated deep, and the ridge of his head stroked her mark where ecstasy laid waiting. The dishes in the cabinets rattled as her shoulders and head rattled the very screws that held them on the wall.

They paid no attention to the glasses and mugs pushing at the cabinet doors, and the occasional one that fell, at each thrust of his hips. He was spreading her wide, going in deep. His thickness pushed at her vaginal walls, and the curvature of his head pressing against that point that brings her to the edge of orgasm; tickling, and teasing her at each long stroke of his cock inside her. He pushed her to the side, laying her down on the counter, knocking over the countertop utensils that lay in her way. Flipping her leg over, her legs came together, and he grabbed her by the shoulder closest to the counter, and grabbed her breast with his free hand. He pushed and he pulled, gripping her breast, slamming his hips against hers. Her posture tightening its grip on his member, she could feel the pressure building. The tissue surrounding her erection being stroked even more. He pressed in, feeling the pressure of her thighs. Running his hand the length of her body, feeling the curve of her hips, the tense muscles in her back, he stroked her neck, pulled back on her shoulder, and slid her off the counter. With one hand on her hips, and the other pushing her down on the counter, his passion pushed deep from behind. Reaching underneath, he grabbed her breast, and leaned forward, trying to fill her deeper, to get himself closer, and feel her even more. Her face slid across the counter at each thrust, her mouth open trying to catch her breath, as she came once again. She could feel him swelling, his thrusting getting faster, his head getting bigger. She felt the throbbing of his cock deep inside her as his passion released, bringing her to orgasm again. She felt his lips on her back, as his strokes slowed to none, but he still remained inside her. Neither of them ventured to move, except for the occasional push, and circling motion, of his hips. The grease from the bacon, sizzled and popped spraying the counter around the stove, and the eggs turned black from neglect, as the smell of passion in the room still dominated. Still lying on the counter, with Brook's body laying on hers, and his lips exploring her neck and back, she didn't open her eyes. "I'll call my friends and tell them I'm not coming."

The Affair

1

It had seemed like an eternity that Tamra spent trying to find her old self; to recover that part of her that the divorce took from her, and what every relationship that followed took from her. Through her struggles she remained in relationships she wasn't happy in, and had done things that she wasn't proud of. But, she always tried not to regret anything, because the things that she did she needed at the time she did them. They helped fill the vacancies in her heart. They helped keep her distracted from her pain, and her insecurities. She would not have survived if she had not had these indiscretions to get her through the hardest of times. Her self-esteem was low, and allowed her to get caught up in a relationship with a narcissistic man who pushed it even lower. He kept her there, as far down as he could, to keep this dream that the world revolved around him alive. She stayed with him, only because deep down she feared she just wasn't as beautiful as she had once been, that she wouldn't find anyone to love her the way she needed to be loved. So she stayed to keep from being lonely. Although at the time, she was already alone emotionally.

It was that situation that began to change her, that would make Tamra open to be preyed upon by another and open her to new things. All alone in her relationship, as far down emotionally as he could keep her; the message she would receive on Facebook would bring a little light into her dark room. He was the brother of a guy she had dated in college. Through Facebook friends they had in common, he had found her, and began his journey to reel her in. He deceived her, but she was letting it happen because she really didn't want to know. His words and compliments made her feel beautiful, and their conversations made her feel wanted. They lived some distance away, but distance was not a concern to her right now. She needed what he was giving her.

While her boyfriend was out of town, she took the opportunity to escape. She hopped on a plane to meet him. He arranged to meet her at a bar around the corner from her hotel. It wasn't long before they were in the parking lot, in the backseat of his car, not even two blocks from where she had a room. She couldn't wait, and neither could he. Throwing her panties to the floorboard, she pulled her skirt up and straddled him right there. Pulling her top down, she pushed her nipple into his mouth. She rode him hard, and quick. The public nature of it added to her excitement.

It wasn't just the act of filling her needs; it was a whole combination of things. He made her feel beautiful, wanted, sexually desired, and alive. He was talented in more than just his manipulation of her; he was talented in the bedroom as well. But she needed all of that. She used that to give her the confidence and strength to walk away from the man who was keeping her down. Her torrid affair didn't end right away. She knew he was married, and she hated herself for needing him; but she did. For over a year she would meet him in parking lots, when he was passing through town, in the family bathrooms at airports, or just the room of her hotel. The risk taking added that much more excitement to the affair. But, there came a time when she came to her senses, and she ended that chapter of her life. It wouldn't end as easily as it should have, and he hounded her relentlessly. It was getting ugly, and her old feelings of low self worth began to creep back in.

    To escape, once again, the dark nature of the depression that lingers dangerously close to feeling down about oneself, she began searching the internet for ways to meet new people. A market flooded with free dating sites, that offered very little, she settled for one. Plenty Of Fish seemed harmless enough, and offered her the opportunity to screen men without having to suffer the bar scene. It was not that she wasn't outgoing. She could go out with friends and pick up men; but, she was just running into a scarce selection of them worth her time to choose from. Restoring her belief in herself, and finding what she needed from a relationship to get her there, was harder than it sounded. She knew she was a great person, and she knew she was just as beautiful outside as she was in; for some cruel reason, nature made it more convincing when a man made her feel it. Made her feel it in the way he looked at her, in the way he touched her, in the way he kissed her, in the notes that he left her or messages he sent her. By some cruel act of nature, these are what she needed to make her feel complete.

In less than twenty-four hours of having her profile for all to see, she had over a hundred messages. After a while, she would weed through a portion of them, the ones that every woman got. The loathing men who simply could not get past their bitterness towards their ex-wife, the freaks of nature who should be arrested simply for stealing oxygen from the air we all breathe, the perverts who for some deranged reason think that their nude photos will get them the woman of their dreams, and the dangerously desperate. As her hopes began to sink with each message she deleted, and each filthy profile she scanned, she found one. His message was different, light hearted, humorous, and uplifting in the spirit of its text. It definitely caught her attention. They messaged back and forth for hours, his messages giving her the laugh she needed. Still holding her insecurities tight, she kept her messages short, not wanting to frighten him away. But, as it turned out, it was her guarded nature that made him feel uneasy. He told her as he continued to joke with her, that what he was really looking for was a woman whose sarcasm matched his, whose humor made him funnier, whose quick wit made for arousing banter. It was somewhat freeing to her, lifting those restrictions she placed on herself in fear that what she might say may turn the conversation sour. She snapped back, before he could close the door on their conversation. That was what she needed, permission to be herself; permission to be a strong, confident woman; recognition that she had that right.

The conversation, after all that uncertainty, changed. Their banter became more playful, and their conversation came easily. She was taken with him and eager to meet, but as Valentine's Day approached, she had already made plans to pamper herself with a trip to Lake of the Ozark's, to be alone. But that wasn't going to keep her from talking to him. She was sure that he was a player, but she didn't really care, and she really didn't want to know. The poetic way in which he wrote his words, laid down his thoughts, and formed his sentences, just made the romantic in her cry out. His thoughts were quick, and effortless. Any initial concerns, of him stealing his words from some unknown journals, were laid to rest quickly. Their quick witted banter so evenly matched, their passion so easily flowing in their written conversation. "Tamra, Tamra, Tamra! Your name alone rolls off my tongue like a passionate kiss……

    Oh how they long for the chivalry of the past.

    Those times when the words "Love You Forever" seemed to last.

    A system of rights, and laws, causing these romances to crumble.

    Decades of lawsuits, and offenses, making the male suitor cautiously stumble.

    All the ceremony gone, flowers wilting in the stores all alone;

    The father's permission no longer needed, daughters all grown;

Now distance becomes the key to finding love without offense;

Hiding behind computers, responses often making no sense;

Awkward ceremony is this, the pressing of the right key;

Dating online, your loneliness for the world to see;

So many get hurt in the world absent romantic pursuit;

Before there is pain, they unplug so the plea is mute;

Somewhere in that exchange, the romance got lost;

In the crowded waves of data, their signals got crossed;

They move on so quickly, to the next romance;

Every time they hit a key, giving love another chance."

"James," she wrote, "plagiarism is just plain wrong!"

"Oh no," he wrote back. "There's no plagiarism here. When I'm with the right woman, the words simply flow like a good wine."

"Well, now wine I can handle! But, it can't be cheap wine; I just won't be having that. So I'm guessing that you like wine?" She quipped.

The sarcastic banter played out through much of the afternoon, as she began to feel more like she was talking to a friend, becoming more open and genuine. It was his humor that she needed, and the passion in his words. She found herself caught in his web, when he combined the two. She had to read his message twice:

"Shouldn't we be serious, and ask serious questions? We are not going to get anywhere if you keep torturing me!!! It could take a very public and disastrous turn.

The Love Connection

Chuck: "Good afternoon, I'm Chuck Woolry, and this is The Love Connection! Today, we are meeting with James, who is back stage, and the lovely Tamra, here on the couch. James, let's start with you! Tell us about the date."

James: "Chuck, let me say, it was very romantic!!! She lives in the middle of nowhere, so options are limited. I packed a large umbrella, blanket, picnic basket full of wine, along with various cheeses, sausages, and crackers. I can't tell you how difficult it was to haul all that up there on my motorcycle. I set us up on this high hill overlooking a beautiful valley, filled with deer and flowers. It was perfect Chuck!"

Chuck: "Was it the perfect setting Tamra?"

Tamra: "That is an exaggeration, to say the least! I was greatly disappointed that he didn't put forward the extra effort to pick a bug free hill. Instead, I had to share my blanket with an entomologist dream picnic!"

Chuck: "Errr, okay Tamra. Tell us about James. What did you guys talk about?"

Tamra: "I don't know Chuck. Men are just a step above Neanderthal on the evolution scale. When they start talking, all I hear is Blah Blah Blah. He was there to pay for my meal...."

Chuck: "Okay Tamra.... So did you have a nice dinner at least?"

Tamra: "Chuck, he brought Jimmy John's sandwiches on the picnic, and he didn't even bring my favorite! How hard is it to remember the Queen B Special?"

Chuck: "Tamra, I don't think they have a sandwich named that."

Tamra: "Yes, they do Chuck! Every time I walk in my local store, they sigh heavily, because they are happy to see me. Then, they call over their shoulder for someone to make the Queen B's Special sandwich!"

Chuck: "I don't think that's what they mean Tamra."

Tamra: "Let me stop you there Chuck. I'm already bored with this conversation. It's time for me to take a break, so I'll be back in 2 and 2...."

Chuck: "Okay, James. That does not sound like such a fabulous date."

James: "Well Chuck. I was told that she was the Ultimate Dream Date, and that if my answer was any different she would hot wax my legs and testicles, and extract my teeth with pliers!......She was the Ultimate Dream Date Chuck!!!!""

You could almost hear Tamra laughing through the phone. "Heyyyyy, I'm not like that at all!!!;-)"

"Yes, you are! LOL. Hold on! Let me finish writing this next one!;-)"

"You are silly!" She replied.

"I said wait, woman!:-) I'm almost done. Stand by……

The Love Connection, Part II

Chuck: "Welcome back, if you are just joining us, I'm Chuck Woolry and this is The Love Connection. Our last couple is returning after a disastrous first date. I should say that there was a difference of opinion on how that last date went – so, we arranged a second date. Let's meet James and Tamra…..(Audience claps). How are you Tamra?" Chuck asks with his usual gleaming smile.

Tamra: "You mean, other than having to talk to you again, Chuck?!?!"

Chuck: "Okay, let's move right over to James. Hello James. To start things off for us, could you explain to the audience why you are sitting behind a dark screen?"

James: "Well Chuck, I'm not quite sure what happened. I've been a very controlled person most of my life. I seem to have lost control of everything, and there are quite a few creditors that are actively hunting me down."

Chuck: "Okay, James. That's understandable. Can you give us an idea of where things took a turn for the worst?"

James: "Well, it seems to have started after my first date Chuck. I don't know what happened, but I just feel like I've been taken advantage of. She does this thing with her fingers, Chuck!"

Chuck: "I see! Tamra, do you feel like you've taken advantage of James?"

Tamra: "No Chuck. I just used him like he wants to use me! While his brain was still trying to figure out how to carve a wheel, I had already built the car to drive it on!"

Chuck: "I'm afraid that you lost me there, Tamra."

Tamra: "Of course I did Chuck! Stay with me here. Try to keep up….. I showed him what he wanted to buy, and he simply did what men do – tried to do whatever he could to get it. I'm an artist Chuck. When I go to sell one of my paintings, I pull at the buyers strings. The moment I see his lips puckering outward, I raise the price. For example Chuck! You guys offered to give James and I a free, all expenses paid, trip to Disney World, if we came back on the show. Did you not?"

Chuck: "Yes. It's a gift we give to our participants."

Tamra: "Do you like the short black dress I'm wearing Chuck?"

Chuck: "Ummm, yes! You look very nice Tamra."

Tamra: "What I like about this dress is how it shows the curve of my inner thigh."

James: "Look away Chuck! Don't do it! Don't follow the fingers Chuck!"

Tamra: "If you run your fingers up the inner thigh, very gently, it almost feels like a man's lips. I can then just circle my finger lightly in the valley where most men wish they could explore."

James: "Look away Chuck! You're doing that kissy Duck Face thingy, Chuck! Look away!"

Tamra: "Now Chuck. Disney isn't very romantic, is it? Wouldn't a week in the Cayman Islands be a much more passionate, erotic, and sensual getaway?"

James: "Say no to the Duck Face Chuck! Say no to the kissy lip Duck Face Chuck!!"

Tamra: "Don't you think Chuck? Wouldn't you feel more passion along the long, smooth, curving beaches of the Caymans Chuck?"

James: "Forget it Chuck! You might as well join me back behind the dark screen!"

"Lmao! You are such a dork! That is not me at all," responding to his text.

"I know! But it sounded funny! So how about we go for that ride, and hit a winery or two?" James knew she would have a hard time turning down a ride, and a winery, all on one date – she loved doing both. It was obvious that there was an imminent connection between them, more so than the one they had already. They fed off each other's sarcasm, quick wit, and sexual banter. They had been doing nothing in the days to follow, but arousing each other's desire, building up that sexual tension, sending each other pictures that don't quite show everything but just enough to make the other person's desire that much stronger.

By the time they had met, James and Tamra had gotten each other so worked up, they were both ready to explode. The sexual tension between them was oozing out, as fast as the beer they were drinking was going in. They met for a quick snack, to hold them over for a while, had a beer, and got to know each other in person. The connection was just as strong in person, as was their excitement to be with each other. He was not everything she was looking for, but he fulfilled those emotional needs that she so desperately struggled with. It was hard for him not to touch her leg while they talked. She wasn't dressed provocatively, but he liked a classy lady who could dress down. Her tight faded jeans, with alternating frayed holes, hugged her body like an extra layer of skin. They perfectly fit her every curve and crease, so that any man that laid eyes upon her, wanted to be those jeans. Her long sleeved soft tan rayon blouse was very form fitting, but classy none the less. Those bright blue eyes of hers leaving him speechless, and her lips just demanding a man's attention; all of his attention, all the passion a man's lips could muster. Her long blonde hair pulled back into a pony tail; she was ready to ride.

During the long ride up Hwy 79, they first stopped for gas in Old Monroe, spending a few more minutes flirting and talking, putting them too much at ease. He helped her with her helmet on, taking every opportunity to brush up against her, touch her face, caress her ear, and feel the softness of her hair against his skin. They saddled his 2003 Harley-Davidson Road King, decked with a little chrome throughout, shined up just to impress. By the time they hit Elsberry, she was clinging to him tighter. The historic vibration of the Harley-Davidson worked hard to weaken her resistance. She loved to ride. North of Louisiana, Missouri, where the hills were at their most scenic, he could feel that she had fully relaxed. Her legs squeezed his hips, an unintended response to the motorcycle vibrating her erogenous zones, getting her aroused. Whenever he talked to her, she leaned forward, pressing her breasts up against his back, and placed her hands along the sides of his thighs. He didn't think he could take much more. In an old scenic rest stop, between Louisiana, and Hannibal, Missouri, he pulled off to show her the view.

When you walk some distance away from the area allotted for parking, the view of the river was spectacular. He took Tamra by the hand, "C'mon, it's beautiful from the edge, a little further in the woods." They stood overlooking the river and valley that held it, watching a Blue Grey Heron glide through the air and skim the water. Her relaxed, playful demeanor made him feel warm. She wrapped her arms around his, resting her chin on his shoulder. Her eyes looked so bright in the sun and her lips so desirable when she curled the upper one up in her sarcastic smirk. He couldn't control himself anymore. Pushing her back against a large tree, he took hold of her by the hair, and then grabbed her jaw running his thumb across her lips. He pressed his lips hard against hers, his tongue to hers, holding that kiss as long as he could before he had to breathe. Moving his lips to her ear, then to her neck, he took hold of her waist. As he moved down her body, tasting her skin, she unbuttoned her blouse. Her pants followed suit. Cupping her breasts, he took her nipple into his mouth attempting to pull all the life it had from it, then the other. As he squeezed her breast, he made his way further down, parting her legs with his jaws.

He kissed her lower lips, caressed the hood of her clitoris with his tongue. She threw her leg over his shoulder, pulling him in, holding him captive. Covering her pleasure with his mouth, he warmed her with the hot air from his lungs. Then, kissing her lower lips, he manipulated them from side to side to make room for his tongue. Probing in and out, side to side, and then taking her clitoris between his lips he could feel she was aroused. Once again, he covered her pleasure with his mouth, and awakened her senses with his hot breath, flipping his tongue from side to side. As he pulled off, he took her clitoris between his lips, and pushed two of his fat fingers between her legs. Tamra cried out. Deep he moved them, then pulling them back till he found the patch of skin where orgasms go to hide. Flicking his fingers back and forth, then circling them over, he teased that place where she wanted him to be. Back and forth he moved his finger tips, telling her to come hither, back and forth he could feel her orgasm rising. He squeezed her breast, sucked gently on her clit, and flicked his fingers to take her to a place she had never been. A world where her pleasure was the most important thing; where her body was the most precious thing.

She could feel her legs go weak, her body start to tingle, and her mind wrapped in a blanket of darkness as the orgasm took control. Her body shook, and a gushing feeling released all tension she had between her legs. He held her up, as she felt the weakness sink in, and then set her down at the base of the tree. Pulling at his jeans, she took his member into her mouth, rolling it across her tongue as it grew in size. Filling her mouth, and spreading her jaws, she massaged it to life. She could feel it harden, stiffen with anticipation, go fully erect in its desire. Grabbing her by the hair, he turned her around, and then down to the ground on her elbows he pushed her; pulling back on her hair to arch her hips upward. He spread her legs with his hands, then her lower lips with the head of his cock. She cried out, losing her breath at each thrust of his hips. He went deeper, spreading her wider. He pushed her head downward, and grabbed her by the hips. Thrusting deep; thrusting hard. Her cries muffled by the leaves she screamed into. Again and again, he pushed, slapping her across the ass to liven up whatever erogenous zones he had missed. She could feel him getting bigger, swelling within her, growing harder. Hitting its mark every time, hard and fast, starting to black out again, she became weak all over again. As she felt his member throbbing inside her, she came once again, and again.

■■

2

They lay there only a moment, with her eyes closed and face in the leaves, and him running his lips down her neck and shoulders. He would pick the grass and leaves out of her hair, as he helped her put her helmet back on. They continued north on 79, with her legs pressed tighter to his, and her arms wrapped around him. Without any real plans, they were just focused on getting in a ride on a beautiful day. As they approached Hannibal, he slowed, turning into Sawyer's Creek. At one time, their food, and especially their pies, melted in your mouth. There was nothing more heavenly than their cheese cake and a cup of their coffee. "Let's get a bite to eat, to get our strength back." James smiled, sliding his helmet strap onto the handlebar.

They ate out on the deck, overlooking the mighty Mississippi River, talked, flirted, and took jabs at each other in the sarcastic banter they both had mastered. Instead of making their way over to the winery at Mark Twain Cave, she wanted to play. So, after grabbing a bottle of wine and some glasses from the wine shop, they readied themselves for a professional round of touch and feel miniature golf. To him, it was wonderful to have a woman who appreciated his affection. He had found that if he focused all his attention on pleasuring the woman that his satisfaction wasn't far behind. Self satisfaction was fleeting, but tending to the emotional and sexual needs of a woman was so gratifying to watch. To watch her lose herself in the moment; watch her cherish every touch, and every kiss; watch her heart, her mind, and her body be lifted to such euphoric pleasure, that she surrenders herself completely, is so much more exhilarating than just punching a time clock in the bedroom. He was all about making foreplay an all day thing; every look, every touch, every kiss, and every note or message he would send.

As she went to hit the ball at the very first hole, he stepped up behind her. "Here, let me give you a professional lesson on the game of golf." He placed his hands on her hips, moved them up her sides to her shoulders, and down the length of her arms. His chest pressed against her back, his warm breath making her neck line tingle, and then he touched the curve in her neck with his lips. "You see, the key to this game is to relax. You're not relaxed." He touched his lips further down, moving along the exposed part of her shoulder. Then, he moved to her ear. "You're never going to beat me, Tamra. You have to know how to caress the ball into the hole. You have to be able to gently stroke all the landscape that surrounds the hole you want to be in. You have to caress the slopes, and the curves, and make it so that the hole opens itself up to you; wanting you inside it; desiring your essence to penetrate its rim, and drop into the depth of what it offers." He moved her hair, caressing her other ear with his lips. "You can't do that unless you relax, and make it the most important thing in your world."

Tamra dropped her club, turned and grabbed him by the back of the neck. "Oh my God! You need to stop!" She shoved her tongue into his mouth. She missed her putt, with his constant distraction. There were eighteen holes for him to torture her, tease her, and touch her. It was the most erotic game of miniature golf she had ever had, and just the way he made her feel made her heart warm inside. He was all about the fun, from the erotic game of miniature golf to childish play of Bumper Boats on the miniature lake. She almost didn't want to leave.

Heading south, he could feel her head resting on his shoulders from time to time. He knew it wasn't because she was tired, because he felt her grip on him tighten as she did it.

Before reaching Clarksville, he turned off on Hwy N. "Let's hit one more winery. There's an old private resort that has a nice view of the fields around it. Crown Valley took over the winery part, I think, not too long ago."

"Okay. I'm game!" She smiled. Running her hands up and down his back, she was getting him aroused again.

For the most part, they hung out at the bar to taste the various wines for the ceremony of it all. It's an unwritten rule when visiting a new winery; you must try their wines first. Otherwise, hit a grocery store to get your fix. After agreeing to disagree, they ended up with two bottles, and made their way out onto the patio where the live band played on. He pulled her out on the dance floor a couple of times, nothing wild, just to the slower music so he could be closer to her. His hands all over her; touching her; running the tips of his fingers down her back, so lightly that she only felt the tingle they left behind. The way she looked at him made him want to dive into her eyes, and never leave. All through dinner, he looked her into the eyes, not hiding the uncontrollable crush he had on her.

They grabbed two more bottles on the way out the door, and he tucked them in his side bags.

"I don't know if I feel comfortable riding back, James. We've both had a lot to drink." She looked worried.

"We're not!" He smiled. "One of the guests, in a group that rented a few studio apartments, left early. I slipped registration $50 to get it cleaned and ready. We are staying the night." He smiled, smacking her across the butt. "You said you didn't have plans, and I've had way too much to drink. Let's go! Get on! It's right over there." A few curves on the private resort road, and they pulled in front of the cabins overlooking the hills. He grabbed the wine, she grabbed the glasses, and he smacked her butt lightly all the way up the stairs. Inside the studio, he placed the wine on the kitchen counter, and pushed her against the counter, the glasses almost breaking as they fell out of her hand and onto the counter. He held her hands on the counter so she knew not to move, as he pressed his body against hers, and kissed her neck. He ran his hands up her arms to her shoulders, pulling the collar of her shirt back a little more, to expose more skin. Her head dropped to the opposite side, giving him more area to move his lips around. She could feel him getting undressed as he kissed her neck, but he stopped her from turning. His hands moved up her shirt, pulling it over her head, then down her shoulders, pressing her hands down on the counter once again. Unfastening her bra, he scratched her back where the strap had been, while his lips moved in a random gentle onslaught of kisses across her skin. He then pushed those scratching, massaging finger tips, around to the front. First arousing the skin by scratching its surface, where the fabric had laid on the skin, then grabbing her breasts firm while he moved his lips up the middle of her back where her muscles paved the way.

 Gripping her earlobe between his lips, he tugged lightly, kissed her shoulder, then kissed and tugged at the ear again, while he pushed her jeans down over her hips. She felt his lips make their way back down along her spine, and his hands grip her buttocks squeezing them firmly to meet his lips.

Placing his hand on the inside of her thigh, he pushed up into her pelvic crease to raise her leg. One pant leg after the other came off, and she was already wet as she could be. He turned her around, reached down grabbing her by the back of her thighs, and lifted her up. Carrying her, he walked over to the couch, a large brown sofa covered in soft fabric, with its back to uncovered windows overlooking the walkways, lake, and fields below. He pushed the coffee table aside with his legs, set her down on the couch and turned her, so her knees were down into the cushions, her arms rest on the back of the couch, and she overlooked the fields. He spread her legs, and pushed the tip of his fully erect cock against her lower lips. He moved it around, teasing her, torturing her, preparing her. He could hear her frustration in her breathing. She breathed out impatiently, and he pulled the tip back out. She felt his thumbs, pushing at her inner thighs, and his lips and tongue begin to work their magic between her legs. She was dying from the anxious excitement he was giving her, wanting him inside her. "Damn it! Stick it in!"

The swollen head pressed against her lips once again, but he wouldn't stick it all the way in. He rolled it around, pressing it against her lips, massaging her vulva, and pressing against her clitoris, he could see her back muscles tense up. He pushed his way in, spreading her lips wide with the girth of his member. The large head of his cock, with its pronounced ridge, pressed in, and aroused sensations along the wall of her uterus. He pushed in deep, and her breath fogged up the window in front of her as she exhaled from the effort. Grabbing her by the hips, he squeezed her by the muscle and fatty tissue alongside it, and he began to pound her repeatedly. With his left hand, he grabbed her right shoulder, and continued with the rapid in and out punishment. Circling his hips, clenching his muscles to shove his shaft deeper, he arched his cock up further. She cried out. She couldn't catch her breath. She cried out. Her head dropped down against the glass, as she tried to catch her breath. He pushed harder. He pushed faster, circling in and around, and tensing to curve it up. Gripping the back of the couch, she raised up, squeezing her hips together, as he thrust himself upon her.

Her breasts up against the window, she caught a glimpse of the couple on the sidewalk below looking up. She didn't care anymore. The shaft of his member throbbing as it pushed its way in and out, the head hitting its mark at each aggressive thrust of his hips, and the rolling movement of his hips brought her closer to that overwhelming rush that rolls through the body like a tidal wave. The wave that hits right before she starts to black out, and feel dizzy. She came. She came again. And, she came again. He lifted her up, and moved her to the bed, kissing her on her shoulder and neck, as she lay there with her eyes still closed.

Fetching the wine and glasses, he pulled back the comforter, and turned on the television. With the volume on low, they sat and relaxed. After several minutes, and wetting his lips with the wine, he took her breast into his mouth. He slid his fingers between her legs, and began to rub her clitoris. Her mouth falling open, she fought to keep her breath in as her abdominal muscles tensed from his touch. In his fingers went, to find that magic spot that brings her joy. She gripped his forearm, as he moved his fingers about, flicking them, and circling them. His attention to her body went on for hours. Even though he had recovered enough to get aroused again, it didn't keep him from tending to her needs. They would stop periodically and watch television, chatting a little in between. But while they were talking, he would feel his passion building for her again, and he would stop her mid-sentence with his lips on hers. That chain of events would go on all night.

In the morning, she showered, while he made coffee. Then he jumped in so that they could get on their way. As he walked from the bathroom to where he had laid his clothes down the night before, he found her lying on the bed with her bath towel covering the private areas of her body. "Damn James! I came so many times yesterday, that I had an orgasm in the shower just thinking about it. Are you like this all the time?"

"It's hard not to be, when a man's with a woman like you!" He kneeled down on the bed, throwing his towel to the side.

Her towel lay on top, showing the contours of her breast, her abdomen, and just covering her pelvic region, before falling off to the side onto the bed. He pinned her by the wrist, and straddled her. "Look at you in all your beauty! That glorious body of yours, lying sheepishly covered by that towel. You are so arousing!" He kissed her lips, her neck, and then ran his tongue down the length of her shoulder pressing his lips against her skin from time to time. The edge of the towel ran along the top of her breasts, with one corner barely covering the full nipple. He outlined the edge of the towel with his lips, kissing the top of her breasts with an open mouth and tongue. He pressed his lips against the cloth covering her breast, till he could feel the outline of her nipple. Then pulling his lips together, he tugged at the nipple and the towel that covered it. Finding his way to the edge again, as the fabric lay wrapping itself around the curve of her breast, he returned to outlining the edge of towel. Around the curve of her breast his lips moved, then down along her side where her body jerked slightly from the tickle. Another corner of the towel came to rest on her thigh and his lips and tongue tickled their way around its edge, down between her thighs. As she started to spread her legs, her breathing becoming heavier, he stopped. His lips moved to reconnect where the towel covered her stomach. He kissed the fabric that covered her so well. Then taking the towel between his teeth, he pulled it down slightly as he watched her breasts come out from underneath.

Giving each breast its much deserved attention, he nibbled at each of them, arousing a squeal from her lips. He moved from side to side, then up to her neck, and back down to the beautiful breasts he held in his hands. When her nipples were rock hard, he knew that he had done enough. Working his way back down the towel, he kissed her thighs along the edge of the towel. Again her legs began to spread, and her breathing became deeper. He tickled her inner thigh with his tongue, and scraped the tender skin between the thighs with his teeth. She spread wide. With the bridge of his nose, he pushed the towel up, finding her pleasure with his lips. His probing tongue pushing the breath from her lungs, and made her chest feel weak. He was down there for what seemed an eternity, never once coming up for air. So masterful he was with his tongue, and so good with his lips, that she never wanted him to stop. If there was ever any question in her mind, he convinced her then that her pleasure was his top priority.

■■

3

When she got home, after he dropped her off at the bar where they had originally met, she plopped down in the chair at her dining room table and went into her POF, Plenty Of Fish, profile to put it in hiding for the time being. As she went through her notifications, and messages, she tried to weed through them to clear her cache. She wasn't interested in any one else at the time, but she didn't want to leave all her messages sitting in her box while she pursued this relationship with James. He was handsome, funny, masculine, and he fulfilled a woman's every sexual or emotionally sensual need. She couldn't see herself walking away from that. But, life never works out like we want it to, or like we plan. While deleting messages, there was one that caught her eye. There was something about him. When she looked at his profile, she just knew there was something there. That instant attraction, and feeling in your gut, when you know something is right. The panic of the circumstances set in. She wanted to be with James, he fulfilled needs that most men could only dream of. He captured her heart with his words, and played her emotions like a violin arousing her deep within.

This man, Richard, was not debonair. She could feel his humility in his look. He was not very good looking, but very easy to talk to, and his profile struck a chord in her. She fell back in her chair. What to do now? She didn't want to lie to James, nor lose him. But, she had this uncontrollable desire to meet this man, and understand the feelings that stirred deep within her. She had to. It would have to work.

James was frequently out of town for work, so he didn't need to know. The conversation she took up with Richard gave her a strong feeling of his good character. He insisted they meet for dinner that night. A little flustered by the demand, since she had only just got back from the winery with James hours before, but she agreed. She had almost hoped that she would not be as attracted to him in person, that she would be checking her watch praying for the night to end. That didn't happen. He was just as comfortable, good looking to her, well mannered, and well dressed as he was in his pictures. They hit it off extremely well. He was a perfect gentleman. As much as she wanted to sleep with him, he kept her virtue in place. In their conversations online, he had joked about taking her on a trip with him and a group of friends. Now that they had met, he mentioned it again, only this time more serious. She wasn't sure what to do.

After days of texting back and forth, she finally broke down and told James that she might be going out of town with a friend the following weekend, but hadn't made up her mind.

She was going to meet with them the following night, and make up her mind. James was so easy to talk to, she found the information slipping right off her tongue, and his understanding eased her mind. "Hey, it is what it is! It always comes in waves. You will have nothing at all for an extended period of time, and then all of sudden you have three people you want to date come at you all at once. If you feel that strongly about your connection with him, I don't want to be the one to interfere. I know how important that connection is. I've spent over a year trying to find it, and when I finally do her feelings are not the same. It's okay Tamra. I understand. I would be lying if I said it doesn't hurt, but I understand. I only wanted to meet one lady, who makes my passion burn, keeps my mind distracted all day long, and invades my peaceful dreams so that my aroused passion wakes me up. Who keeps me aroused and feeling passionate all day long! I have met that woman, Tamra; to me there is no doubt. Although you don't feel the same burning passion for me, your beauty still stirs me deep down and makes my words flow like wine!"

"Oh James! I don't know what to say. I don't want to hurt you in any way. But, I just know I have to see this through to find out. I may not like him as much the second date. That happens quite a bit. And, I have not agreed to go away with him yet." She clicked send, feeling her heart sink. The stress this situation was placing on her was tearing her apart.

"It's okay, Tamra! No worries!" James swallowed any hope he had, and took a deep breath.

The following day, James could not hold back any longer, knowing that she may not contact him if Richard didn't work out. His heart sunk when she messaged that the man still held her passion, and that she would be going away with him for the weekend. The spontaneous nature of it added excitement to it for her. She continued to text James, despite making up her mind, which told him that she was still torn inside. He began to sense that he, James, was what she wanted in a man, but this Richard was what she needed. Richard was wealthy, refined, and sociable. He often traveled to remote areas to meet with friends, and liked having the company of a companion. She needed that sociable lifestyle, and the luxury that he offered. It filled her heart with comfort, knowing she didn't have to worry about things. That everything would be taken care of. She could be surrounded by beautiful things, and that made her feel beautiful and glamorous herself. Too much of a lady, she didn't post pictures of him on Facebook, but James was still tormented by her updates. He had fallen for her something hard. It was something that he had not expected and out of character of his normal ability, to just walk away. But he couldn't turn away, checking her posts, happy that she was having fun, but saddened that it wasn't with him.

He kept his promise to avoid sabotaging her time with this man, even though she wanted to remain friends. As a gentleman, he was not going to text her; but, that didn't keep him from checking his phone to see if she had messaged him. He had sabotaged her weekend, without knowing it. That battle within her over her needs, and her wants, was not likely to go away anytime soon. It tormented her. Richard was a great man, and everything she needed a man to be at moments in her life. They had hung out with his friends, having a great time. He took her to places she had never been. And he made her feel relaxed when she was with him. She had no reservations about him. The first night they spent in Nashville, they stayed out late with friends, soaking up the Nashville night life. When they got back to their room, they began to kiss, and it was comfortable like an old shoe. They had both been drinking, so she tried not to set her expectations too high. But, she did worry, that he may not be the complete package that she had hoped for. As shallow as she felt for thinking it, she was a very sexual person, and needed that to completely give herself over to one man. He was okay, but he was also drunk.

The next morning, Richard stepped from the shower to find her lying on the bed, with only a towel covering her body from just above the nipples to just below that desirable gap in her thighs. "Hey!" He smiled, tapping her leg. "We need to get dressed, and get down there to breakfast. My friends are meeting us in the restaurant." Tossing his towel on the bed, he began to get dressed.

■■■

4

By the middle of the week, James had given up hope. Then his phone lit up with a message. It was from her. "Hey, how are you? Did you go on any hot dates?"

"No. I was still drinking away my sorrows from the last one who walked out of my life!:-)" He messaged back, half joking, and half not. The sarcasm was always good between them. She obviously wanted to talk.

"I'm sorry! I know you must hate me!" she replied.

"No. I really do understand. As the renowned poet Salina Gomez once sang, "The heart wants what the heart wants!" And, there is nothing but truth in that. I hope you had a great weekend with him." Again, it was mostly half truth on his part.

Although he had wanted to feel that happiness, he knew that you couldn't force that happiness on anyone.

"It was pretty good! I did have fun, really. He is a perfect gentleman, and I like all his friends. I'm glad I went. I think I needed that."

James: "So, there is no chance of running away and eloping anytime soon?:-)"

Tamra: "You're a dork! He's a great guy! You are too! Don't ever think that you don't hold a place in my heart. I've never met a man who is so unselfish with his passion."

James: "But, you didn't say No either!;-)"

Tamra: "James, you are silly. I'm seeing him tonight, and then he was talking about meeting friends this weekend."

James: "You still didn't say No!;-)

Tamra: "Ugh! Lol... You are adorable!"

James: "I KNOW, Right!!!;-)"

Tamra: "LOL"

James: "He cometh on his knees, with roses in hand;

    Across the distance between them, the great divided land;

    Fighting great battles through the kingdoms between them;

    His chivalrous journey to capture her heart defeats him."

Tamra: "Awe! You do not make this easy at all."

James: "It's okay Tamra. It wasn't that good. (Tap, Tap, Tap) I think my Shakespeare App is broken!;-)"

Tamra: "Still. It was sweet."

    You would have thought that there was no Richard between them. She continued texting him while she was at work, thoroughly enjoying and needing how at ease he put her. His words still aroused her emotion, teasing her from a distance although he claimed it was all harmless. No more harmless than her inability to let go of him, and stop texting him. That next Saturday morning, she told him that she had to let him go because Richard was picking her up. They were heading to The Wine Country Gardens in Defiance, MO, for a company group event. Nestled quietly on a 42 Acre farm, with a century old two story house, with an amazing view, as its centerpiece for its atmosphere, it had retained a respectable reputation, and tended to host a large number of corporate events. He almost wished that she had not let him know, and would leave him out of these updates on the progress of her relationship with Richard. But, she just couldn't seem to let him go, as much as she wanted to; and, he couldn't put it to an end.

She and Richard had grabbed brunch before headed down into Missouri wine country, and met up with his associates some of which she had met in Nashville. They were a really fun group, and felt so comfortable and like she fit in with this group. She was happy. They had been sitting on the North Patio, watching the sun rise up overhead, lighting up the valley below. You could not ask for more beautiful of weather. She kept her legs out from under the table, hoping to give them a little more sun, the rays beating down on them warming her exposed arms in her sleeveless pullover top.

Richard was having a good time, conversing with his friends. She did like seeing him smile; he was such a good guy. Tamra stood, "Well, I'm going to go grab myself another glass of wine, and try something new. I'll be right back."

"Hey! Grab me another glass too!" Richard handed her his glass, turning back to his friends. "Thanks babe."

She took his glass, and headed up the patio steps, when she saw the gathering near the tasting room and buffet set up for the event, she veered right, cutting through the trees, to go around the old house to the other side, to get to the bar. It was here that she ran into James.

"James! You can't be here!" She was startled, stopping in her tracks.

"C'mon! " He grabbed her by the elbow, leading her off to the side of the old building, where two single bathrooms sat. He pulled her in, shutting the door behind. Taking her by the back of the hair, he pulled her into the corner, where her lips willingly surrendered to his. He could tell that her lips were missing the passion; he could tell that she needed his touch. Their lips held in lock, he moved his hand between her legs and lifted the tips of his fingers up. She moaned, and her breath became erratic. "Get your shorts off!"

She tossed the glasses in her hands into the sink, and pulled at the button on her shorts, kicking them off to the side. He pulled her by the back of her hair, grabbing her by the chin; he pressed his tongue to hers, his lips to hers. He held that passion for a minute, moving his hand down her neck, and the front of her body till he could feel the warmth between her legs. Pushing at her thigh, he lifted her leg over his shoulder to give his lips more room. Her thighs tasted sweeter than before. She smelled more desirable than before. He covered her thigh with his kisses. He marked his territory with his tongue. He took her lower lips between his, first kissing, and then gently pulling on them. He covered her pleasure with his mouth, warming her with his hot air; then moved right into the most passionate of French kisses to her clit. He wanted it. He owned it. There was no man that could bring her the pleasure that he did. The moment her stomach muscles began to pull in, and her chest was releasing all the air she tried to hold in, he pulled out to tease her further. Her thighs tasted so good. The skin that lies between her legs seemed so soft to his tongue, to his wanting lips. They demanded his caress. They cried out for his attention. He could feel it in the movement of her thighs as she pushed them against his face. His lips pressing deep into her valley, as she gripped his hair pulling him in.

She cried out when she exhaled, drawing attention from those passing by outside. She covered her mouth, reminding herself not to scream, trying to muffle what she could not control. Each probe of his tongue sending nervous waves up her spine, and causing her abdominal muscles to contract as she skimmed the edges of a gushing orgasm. Her legs growing weak, more of her weight falling on his shoulders, he didn't slow down. She could feel the movement of his lips, and the flipping of his tongue. Gripping his hair to hold on, she felt lightheaded and tingling throughout her body. Her muffled screams breaking the silence, and echoing off the walls of the tiny room. She felt herself collapsing, as she came. His teeth pushing against her pelvis, and his jaws holding her steady, he kept his pursuit steady. She came again. He rose up, grabbing her by the hair again, leaning her upper body over the sink that stood before them. Still feeling numbness between her legs, she felt his cock push its way in. The mirror above the sink rattled on the wall just a bit, and the pipes below the sink could be heard loosening as well. The woman in the adjoining bathroom was at first shocked, and feeling like her privacy was being violated. But where was she to go. After several minutes of listening to the pounding of the sink on the wall, the vibration of the pipes due to the steady and aggressive motion, and the mirrors, in both bathrooms, being shaken off the wall, she found herself getting aroused. Tamra's groans only became louder. Her moans only became more sensual. Her breathing became more rapid and heavier in disturbing the silence. The lady found herself masturbating to the symphony of passion playing out in the bathroom next door. That symphony ended with a storm of percussion cymbals crashing together.

When James exited the bathroom, he closed the door behind him. The few people that were standing nearby looked at him. One guy lifted his glass of wine in recognition. He turned, heading around the front, to the parking lot. A couple minutes later, Tamra exited the bathroom, not looking at anyone standing near the bathrooms, and walked back to her group. She set the empty glasses on the table and sat down.

"Where's the wine?" Richard laughed.

"Oh. Sorry! I had to use the restroom, and forgot." She was nervous, not really knowing how to act. Her and Richard were only dating, and had not fully committed to anything, yet she still felt like she was cheating on him. But, the passion and exhilaration she felt in that bathroom was hard to dismiss.

■■

5

James waited, not pressuring her for anything. He knew she couldn't help but write him, there was something still there. "I can't James!" She responded, having contacted him first. "I can't just walk away from this. It has nothing to do with you; there is something that just draws me to him. The sex is uneventful, I know. He doesn't have your passion, that's true. And, I don't want to lose you as a friend."

That conversation never stopped, while she continued to work through her struggles. All week long she messaged him talking about what he bought her, and the places that he took her. It was as if she was venting about her confusion, trying to work it out in her head, only needed to hear it out loud. The torment became excitement. The friendship became more of a game. She needed Richard, but wanted James. He was beginning to see how the taboo nature of it all was exciting her. It became more evident, when she messaged him with a harmless message, to tell him that she was going to be at Richard's Lake Condo for the weekend, and she hoped he found himself a "Hottie" for the weekend. Several hours later, he received the message ping, showing her location. He thought it over, but felt it may be better to stay away.

On Friday, Tamra and Richard arrived at the lake. She threw on her bathing suit, and headed down to the dock. Richard was catching up on some work on his laptop, sitting out on the screened in patio. She soaked up some sun, and he got some work done. They gave each other their space. A little later, they hit a show on the strip in Osage Beach, and then grabbed some dinner. He threw some logs in the fireplace for some ambiance, and they sat out on the back patio sipping wine as the sun set across the lake. There is nothing more beautiful than the orange sky of a setting sun, reflecting off the water. She leaned over giving Richard a kiss, running her hand up his leg, with a sensual submissive smile to get him aroused. "Did you want to go to the bedroom?" He smiled.

"Okay!" she said, holding back her desire to just do it right there on the patio.

He grabbed her hand, and led her inside. In the bedroom he got undressed, and lay down on the bed. Tapping the sheets beside him, he encouraged her to join him. As soon as her hip hit the sheets, and her head the pillow, he began to kiss her neck. He moved to her nipple, and placed his hand down between her legs. He moved over top of her, placing a knee on each side. Placing his hand behind her neck, he urged her to get it wet. She sucked on his manhood, making him even harder. When enough saliva had been laid, he moved down between her legs and pushed himself in. She lay there obediently, while he worked his excitement out. It went on for several minutes, and she began to feel herself approaching arousal herself; but, then she felt him cum. He lay on top of her for a moment, still pumping his hips till he was soft. He kissed her with all the passion he could muster, and rolled over. He grabbed his glass of wine, and handed her hers. "Do you want to watch TV?"

"No. If you don't mind, I'd like to go back out and sit on the deck and look out upon the water." She forced a smile.

"Okay, works for me. You might as well enjoy it while you are here." He lifted his glass, and cocked his head with a smirk.

Sitting out on the deck, sipping her wine, she looked out upon the water. Her phone held loosely in her hand, lying on her lap, not lighting up. Still, she checked it to be sure, but there were no messages. She scrolled through some of the previous messages James had sent, to remind her of his charm. Looking at her phone, she waited for a message to appear. Several minutes and a glass of wine later, she checked again. There was still no message. Putting her phone on the table, she allowed herself to set hope aside.

The next morning, Richard and she went out on the boat, and met with some friends of his. She loved all of his friends, and the company that he kept. They spent the day, or much of it, socializing with friends, hanging out, and drinking wine on boats tied together. Later that afternoon, they parted ways with his friends, and headed back to the condo. When she had come out from the bedroom, he was already on the laptop sitting on the deck. She leaned against the frame of the sliding glass door. "Did you want to go back out? I changed suits." He turned to find that she had changed from the red swimsuit she had been wearing, to a new blue swimsuit.

"Hey, looks good. I like it. I'm sorry babe; I need to finish up on these charts." He tapped his fingers on the keyboard of his laptop.

She made her way down the walkway of the dock, past the dock slips, and out onto the open sun deck. As she laid her towel out on the dock, she saw movement. She thought she saw James, but the shadow stepped between two boats. She approached cautiously, calling his name. When she peered between the boats, James stood at the end of the platform. Tamra walked up behind him, resting her forehead between his shoulders. "Why are you here, James? This can't happen."

"You know why I am here." He turned facing her. She was beautiful as ever. The dark blue, two piece bathing suit she wore, fit her perfectly. It cut down just below her muscle flattened tummy, drawing attention to her most prized possession lying between her thighs. The breast cups of her top covered a little over half of her breast, the edge of the material at her cleavage, crossed at an angle up past the edge of her nipple, allowing for much of the curve of her breast to be exposed. It hugged at her breasts, pulling the material tight against her skin. Her nipples were visible to tease any man who looked upon them, if only by the outline pushing through. The suit matched her bright blue eyes. She looked gorgeous. All he could do is stand and look at her.

Grabbing her by the shoulders, he turned her, scooped her up underneath the legs. He threw her legs over the side, and into the Sea Ray Sundancer that sat up on the boatlift beside them. He jumped up into the boat, placed his hands along her side, and guided her into the belly of the boat. Pulling her into the cabin, he pressed her up against the cabinets, at the base of the steps. He looked into her eyes, with his thumb pressing against her lips. Oh how he adored those soft blue eyes. Losing all self control, he fell into those eyes, and his lips pressed against hers with all the hope of feeling every crease in their skin. He cupped the sides of her face, holding her jaw steady, not wanting to let her lips go. Touching, and then tickling her earlobes with his fingers tips while he held her kiss captive. Then he moved them along the sides of her head, making her scalp tingle as they made their way around back. Their lips parted, and their tongues pressed together ever so gently. The two of them irreversibly lost in the moment, their lips feeling perfectly matched to each others' shape. They could feel the passion in each others' heart beat through the tongues that bound them together.

He kissed the ear that he had been stroking, and pressed his lips firmly against her neck. Moving slower than he ever had before, wanting his lips to remember every inch of her body. The fear was setting in that he was really losing her, despite the powerful passion the two held for each other.

He slid the bathing suit straps along her shoulders, and down her arms, as he walked his lips along behind. Taking her face between his hands once again, he pressed his lips to hers, and his tongue to hers, and then slid a hand around behind her back to unfasten the top. It fell down her arms and to the floor. Her full, and firm, beautiful breasts hang unprotected between them. He cradled the one in his hand, as he lowered his head to take possession between his teeth. Rolling the nipple, as he bit down gently, he closed his mouth onto it. Squeezing the breast between his fingers, he opened his mouth wider to take in more of its bounty, and he clamped down upon it pulling it in as he breathed. Then he took liberty with the other.

Sliding his hands down her hips, he pulled her bottoms to the floor. He turned her, sliding his hand down her tummy, and between her legs. His lips to her ear, to her neck, and to her shoulder, he worked his fingers up in. As her breathing got heavier, so did his. As her passion became more heated, so did his. Unbuckling his pants, he let them fall to the floor, kicking one leg free. He moved her over to the bed at the front of the cabin, just below the windows. Moving her knees onto the bed, he slipped in behind. Their heads touching the ceiling, she put her hands on the window frames in front of them. With his tongue in her, she cocked her head to the side, looking out through the white semi-sheer curtain at the boats across from them. She jolted as he joined them together, her buttocks pushing back to meet him. She gripped the window sill as he put the boat in motion. The creaking of the boatlift getting louder, the faster he went. Her panting was getting heavier, and her high pitched grunts getting louder. Suddenly he slowed his pace, but did not stop, and covered her mouth to muffle her cries.

Richard walked out along the dock, to bring Tamra her phone. The rocking of the Sea Ray Sundancer caught his attention, and he looked at it thinking it odd, as he walked by. It must have been an isolated wave, he thought. He was sure Tamra had come down to the dock, and walked around holding her phone up as if that would help find her. Stepping on the sun deck, at the end of the dock, he picked her towel up off the solid platform decking. As several large speedboats had raced by, a series of waves began to make their way in. The dock started lifting and falling, and the boats started rocking. But one boat in particular, was rocking heavier than the rest.

James rocked his hips with the motion of the water, grabbing a hold of her shoulder and a hip, as her hands holding the window frame steadied them both. It took everything she had to keep from screaming or breathing too heavy. She wanted James to stop, but at the same time she really didn't. Somewhere between panic and fear, she found excitement, as she watched Richard walk past the windows of the boat. When he turned to look at the windows of the boat, her heart stopped, but James didn't. The boat rocking with the waves at an awkward angle, side to side, then against the waves as the nose dipped down and up once again. Deep down it went, then arching up. The boats lift screaming out, as the boat thrust upward again and again. She watched

Richard lift his chin, like he was in deep thought, turn, and walk away.

As they both got dressed, and exited the boat in case the owner showed up, she told him that it had to stop. She loved them both, and they were equally good men. But, she believed she was meant to be with Richard. There was that instant connection with him. He did not have the passion that James had, but there was a part of her heart that said he was the one.

■■■

6

When she got back to the condo, she had to explain to Richard that she had gone for a walk. While undressing to jump in the shower, Richard entered the room visibly admiring her body. She always needed that, since she did not see her body in the same way. He placed his hand around her waist, sliding his hand down to take her butt cheek in his hand, and squeezed. They kissed. He ran his fingers alongside her face, and smiled. "Go get your shower. The show starts here in about an hour, and then we'll grab some dinner afterwards." He smacked her butt and smiled.

Despite the things that bothered her, she did adore him. When he wasn't wrapped up in his work or friends, he made her feel wanted and appreciated. She wanted more than what he could offer, but she was willing to try and fight those demons on her own. He was outgoing, fun, affectionate, and masculine. She felt secure with him, and taken care of. Another variety show marked off the list, but they always tried to keep it new and interesting down at the lake. Dinner was difficult. She tried to be attentive, and affectionate towards Richard, but spent more time thinking about James while she tossed her food around on her plate. She was distant, not that he would really notice. When they got back to the condo, she stood at the dresser, removing her earrings and necklace he had bought her earlier in the week, placing them at the base of the mirror. Richard walked up behind her, placing his hands on her shoulder, and began kissing each shoulder back and forth up to the neck. He slid the straps of her dress towards her shoulders, placed his fingers under her chin and kissed her on the lips. He looked her in the eyes, smiled, and stepped back unbuttoning his shirt. He tossed his pants and underwear on the chair, in the corner near the bed, and climbed in waiting for her to join him.

She climbed in, pushed the comforter down so his waist was unobstructed, and took his dick into her mouth. After very little effort, he was erect and pushing on her shoulders for her to lay back. He kissed her lips, and then took her nipple into his mouth sucking on it momentarily before moving to the other. With his duty to her done, he moved to between her legs, and sought to redeem his manhood. Although she did not cum, he seemed to pay it no mind or block out the fact that he did not ever give her an orgasm. It would shatter his ego if he did. He loved her, and she loved him enough not to tell him.

The next morning they sat out on the screened in deck. The condominiums in The Falls Condominiums had several layouts. Theirs was more relaxing and open. As soon as you walked through the front door, you were looking at the dining area, living area with fireplace, and at the screened in deck. The bedrooms were off to the right, at least in their unit. The only available storage, other than closets, was the small storage room on the covered deck. It was not really meant for full time living quarters, just vacation accommodations. He got up, made coffee, while she exited the bedroom in a robe, and opened the sliding glass door to the deck. He brought her coffee, and they sat chatting about their plans for the day. He would set his work aside, get the boat ready, and they would spend the day making rounds to his friend's places on the lake along with a little swimming and skiing. It was a very comfortable and relaxing time on the deck. After drinking coffee, and watching the sun rise across the lake, he got up to get ready. They donned their suits, and went about their self assigned responsibilities. As he walked out the front door, she told him that she would grab the life jackets and be right down.

On the enclosed deck, she stood in the storage closet, undoing knots that someone else had left in one of the ropes. She heard the front door close. Aggravated that he was so absentminded unless it had to do with work, she drug the rope with her as she untied it. "Did you forget the keys to the boat?" She stood in the open sliding glass door, and looked through the open room. She didn't see him. Suddenly, James appeared from the master bedroom, immediately off to the left. "James! What are you doing?"

In less than two long strides, he grabbed her by the neck, and pressed his lips to hers. He moved her out onto the deck, and back against the wall. His hands holding her along each side of her jaw, he kissed her like he was going to lose her. Pressing her against the wall, he could feel her submitting. He moved his hands down along her body, pushing her swim bottoms down her waist, as he reunited with her lips. His fingers between her legs, to find her already wet from him just being there. Lowering himself down, he put his lips and tongue to quick work. It was less than fifteen seconds and he had her cuming uncontrollably. It was the mental arousing, not just the physical stimulation. He slid his arm up the back of her leg, so the back of her knee rest in the cradle of his elbow, and he squeezed her buttocks with his hand. Then he moved the other arm into place, her arms wrapped around his neck, and he lifted her up against the wall. Reaching down between her legs, she could not position his hardened cock any faster to get him in. She felt the pain, the dropping down on it, stretching her further than she would normally be. The force of his upward thrust making him feel so much larger, like he was ripping her open. Her back against the wall, she wrapped her wrists around his neck, leaning back for his next push upward.

The wall was beginning to scratch her back, but she didn't care. It was the motion, and the passion that she desired. Her feet bouncing in the air as he pounded her into the wall, she tried curling them just a bit to keep them from moving so much so she could focus on the movement inside. She pushed her breast into his mouth, squeezing his head tightly, while he moved one arm around her waist to hold her in tighter. Her upper back against the wall again as he tilted her slightly to get a deeper push. She cried out as he began hitting his mark, a place that had been neglected last night with Richard, a place that was always neglected with Richard. As wet as she could be, as wet as she always was with James, she came and then came again. Her head fell onto his shoulder as he continued punishing her, for not being his. Feeling dizzy, and feeling like she was going to cum again, she looked out upon the lake. She wondered if anyone was watching. There were construction workers working around a house just across the small cove they were in. If she had screamed out, they would hear her, but their view would be skewed by the screen of the deck. But, they could still see. Any person sitting at their kitchen table, in the houses across the way, would have a clear view, and a cheap pair of binoculars would give them a front row seat. It seemed to excite her.

As her body tingled, and her muscles tensed, she looked down on two men fishing in the cove. One looked up in her direction, she was sure he was watching. She couldn't see his eyes, but the bill of his ball cap was titled up towards her, and the tip of his fishing pole had begun to dip down into the water unsupervised. She came again. Fading, while her body absorbed the rush, she observed Richard walking out from under the roof of the dock, and up the walkway towards the condo. He looked up, and right at her, so she thought. "Richard's coming!" She whispered her panic in his ear. James continued, he was not going to let that stop him. He pushed harder, the wall digging hard into her back now. A couple of minutes had already passed. "He's coming!" She cried again softly in a panic.

"So am I." He responded. She could feel his pace change, the pulsating of his member deep inside her. She came again.

James lowered her feet to the ground, and pulled up his pants. She pushed him into the storage closet on the deck where she had been pulling stuff out from. The blinds on the front door rattled as Richard opened the door. Grabbing the towel laying on the chair, she wrapped it around her waist and scooped up her swimsuit bottoms just as he walked out. "Are you ready?"

"Yes! I just need to go to the bathroom first. Let's go."

"What happened to your back? It's all red." Richard placed his hand on her shoulder, turning her slightly to look at the large patch of red scratch marks from the cedar siding.

"You weren't around, and my back itched. I scratched it on the wall, while I tried to undo these knots. Here," she picked the rope up off the ground, and pushed it into his chest. "Take this down to the boat, and I'll be down in a minute." She waved her hands scooting him off the patio, shutting the patio door behind her.

"What do we need this for?" Richard looked at the knotted up rope.

"It's just in case we need it. Now go!" When she had re-emerged from the room, where she had put her suit bottoms back on, Richard was still standing there, messing with the knots. Out the door she rushed him with the rope dragging along behind, before James came popping out to see if anyone was there.

■■■

7

James seemed to have become obsessed with the fact that he could not own Tamra completely, but she struggled with recognizing it. She loved him. He just kept showing up wherever she and Richard seemed to be, more and more. The passion and excitement in their sexcapades was exhilarating, so she found it near impossible to refuse his advances. To help control it, she began to delay responding to his texts. It was an unbearable burden on her shoulders knowing that there was a text from him, and to keep from responding back. It would give her extreme anxiety whenever she texted someone and they didn't text back, or in mid-conversation they seemed to stop and not respond till hours later. She knew that would infuriate him, but she just needed him to slow down.

 He would hound her with texts till she responded. Although she tried to keep her responses short, he always seemed to be able to get her to tell where she was. The timing was never convenient, but that was part of the excitement in some cases. Then, after they had their fling, James would walk away like he had possessed her. He had become more distant, the longer the affair went on. It was all "Oh baby, oh baby," before sex, then it was all "you need to just stop seeing this other guy." It became worse after she moved in with Richard. She felt the fact that Richard had money, made James even more jealous. He was almost okay with just having flings with her, but perhaps he felt he was losing his grip on her once she moved into Richard's life completely. The house was larger than she had ever lived in, five bedrooms, large areas for people to gather at parties, an entertainment area downstairs, and a large in ground pool.

With his lake condo on top of all that, she was living a dream. What he had to offer in her happiness, in her mind, equaled the passion James had to offer.

It had been almost a month since she heard from James, when walking along the path on the St. Charles River Front. The Festival of The Little Hills had taken over Old Town Main Street, and the River Front Park. Richard was talking to one of the vendors, in the re-enactment village that was put closer to the woods and the Lewis and Clark Statue, going over details of historical points. He liked the debate, and when it came to history he could get lost in discussion for hours. As she stood patiently beside him, she looked between the two tents off to her right, to find James standing between them. He just stood looking at her, then glancing over at Richard. Her heart jumped. His angry messages had given her strong reason to believe that he would create a scene, embarrass her beyond repair, and destroy what she had with Richard. She told Richard that she was going to look at something, and would be right back.

Walking around behind the tent, she grabbed James by the arm, pulling him out of view. "I'm sorry James! I know I haven't responded to all of your texts, but I've been busy. I don't want to lose you, but I don't want to lose Richard either. The two of you complete me."

"You need to just give him up, or you will lose me. I'm not going to share you with another man anymore, Tamra." Taking her chin into his hand, he ran his thumb along her jaw line.

"What do you want me to do James? You fuck me, then run off and disappear for weeks at a time. I can't just wait around for you, and be available only when you are horny. That's not fair to me. Please don't do this. What we have is perfect! You give me everything he does not. You make me feel everything he does not. You fill a need that he cannot. But, he gives me everything you cannot."

James grabbed her by the arm, pulling her into one of the re-enactment tents that stood open and unattended next to them. They could hear Richard still debating on the other side. He pulled her close, locking her lips down with his, as he wrapped his arm tightly around her waist. Then, spinning her around, he threw her down on the bear skin that cover the floor to the right of the door. Pushing her down on the hide, he threw up her dress, and ripped her panties down. Hurriedly he pulled at his belt, and pushed his pants down. She cried out just a little, as he stuck his cock between her legs. As close as they were to the tents opening, she could see the crowds of people walking by, and she was sure if they had looked hard enough they would see her. At each wave of the motion he created, she felt the circling waves in the river ahead. Through the people, she could see the trees bending from the wind, leaves flipping with the music from the orchestra that played on the distant stage, and the sounds of nature that surrounded it all.

While he pushed, she felt his hands gripping her hips tight, and his cock feeling more angry and harder than it ever had. He drove her face into the fur, and it was all she could do to not scream. She could hear Richard on the other side of the deer skin wall, discussing the transition from frontier to the migration of entire families. She felt James pounding her from behind, while Richard spoke in her ear. This was the closest and riskiest sex they had ever had. Her heart pounded. She looked out upon the groups of people walking by. The fire several feet from the tent, with its flames flickering upward, warming whatever brewed in the cast iron pot that hovered above it. James continued to push in deep, and she gripped the bear skin pulling it to her mouth to cover her grunts. A man stepped between the tent and the fire, several feet from them, and poked at the logs to get more flame. Then he sat down. A rush of anxiety rolled through her, having Richard on one side of the tent, and now this man just outside the opening. Her anxiety fueling her arousal, she was so wet. James pushed, and pushed, reaching up and grabbing her shoulder to complete the control and push in deeper.

She felt a euphoric wave of tingling roll through her body, with her eyes closed, her back arching as her abdomen was sucking in, and she heard Richard thank the man he was talking to. Then she heard his voice again, only closer. She opened her eyes, to see him standing near the opening of the tent, talking to the man seated by the fire. Shoving the bear hide into her mouth, she felt herself starting to cum. Her breathing simply stopped, and she pushed against James' rapidly pumping hips. She came. Then she came again. James continued, while she lay savoring the darkness and streams of thin white lines of light that flashed across it, her thoughts were simply drowned by the gushing release. His cock throbbing as he released his passion inside her. He continued rocking his hips, her face buried in the hide as she listened to Richard just outside the tent door. The man at the fire stood up, encouraging Richard to follow him so he could see what they were talking about.

    James, pulled out, zipped up his pants, pushed her at her hips. She hadn't moved, still feeling the rush, as James stood up. "There you go bitch! We're done! You can have your man!" Falling to the side, she looked at James as he ducked down, making his way out of the tent.

He wouldn't return her texts, or her calls. Then, he finally just blocked her all together.

∙∙

8

After James had finally broken it off, she took it hard. It was her inability to make up her mind that irritated him, and that passion turned to anger. His anger and anxiety frightened her. When passion turns dark, it tends to turn very dark. She tried to keep her emotions from Richard, spending a lot of her time crying in the bathroom, or on long walks that day. Calling in sick at work the next day, she tried to get her head on straight. It was not easy by any means. She was in so much pain. It was such an emotional roll-a-coaster, that she couldn't shake the feeling that she lost something she will never find again. There had been strong feelings between them. The way that he touched her made her feel wanted. The way that he kissed her made her feel desired. The way that he looked at her made her feel beautiful. The way that he constantly showered her with affection made her feel loved. There was so much passion in everything he did. But his passion was also going to be her downfall. He controlled her with it. She knew that if they had continued on that path, she could lose everything she had worked towards at work and in her personal life. And, she recognized that most of their passion existed simply because they were not together. He liked the challenge. He liked controlling her. He liked the sex without any of the responsibilities that come with a relationship. No matter how many times she reasoned through it, it was still tearing her apart because that passion had become her drug. She loved Richard, and all that he gave her, but he lacked passion. James was set on destroying what she and Richard had. The pain was unbearable, and she needed for it to go away. She needed to break the control he had on her. Scrolling through her phone, she looked for any friend that she could call that she knew would be available to talk to. She needed to get out of the house, breathe some fresh air, and get her mind off of things.

Evan was about the twentieth person she called, but he was available when others were not. He was not exactly her first choice in a friend to confide in, because he had only scattered relationships over the years. He was harmless, and a nice guy, but just not appealing enough for women to drop everything and chase after. She always felt sorry for him, because he was so nice. When he said he was leaving work early that day and heading home, she told him she'd pick him up at his house and buy lunch. Of course he agreed. When she arrived, she just shook her head. She should have taken him shopping instead. His striped, short sleeve, dress shirt seemed one size too small. The buttons ready to pop where the fabric stretched around his rounded belly. He wasn't obese, he just had a large belly; it just looked like he didn't try to exercise much, and sat in front of the television eating all the time. The belt curved under the weight of his belly hanging down, keeping his belly from pushing the jeans down. He was cute, and kind of adorable in a comfortable cuddly sort of way - just not a lot of confidence in his step. He was a good friend, listening to her ramble on all through lunch. She could see his face flush a little when she talked about the sex. Not exactly looking uncomfortable with the conversation, but looked a little awkward and shocked by her talking about it so vividly. The more in detail she went, the more he shuffled in his seat not really knowing how to respond.

His face was just blank when she started to cry, and talking about how she worried how she would make it without the passion he gave her, the orgasms he gave her, his cock up inside her, and the thrill of the rush she got in some of the places that he would just bend her over without a care in the world. The more she talked, he could see the more she got herself all worked up and crying. There was not anything he could really say or do, other than to let her talk. Evan went ahead and paid for the meal, and placed his hand on her back trying to awkwardly comfort her as they walked back to the car. She was beside herself, and he wasn't too sure it was a good idea for her to drive. He took the keys, and opened the door for her. All the way back to his house, she cried. Moments of anger and frustration poured out. He just sat silent and drove. It became more awkward as he pulled in his driveway. She had calmed down, so he was sure that she was okay to drive, but felt awkward just waving goodbye. He stood at the front of the car, not sure what to say or do, while she remained seated in the passenger seat for a minute, wiping her tears. She finally exited the car, walked past him, and made her way up the sidewalk. "Can I use your bathroom?"

"Sure!" Evan scurried up the sidewalk past her, getting the door.

Tamra looked around the house a bit. "This is a cute place Evan." Then she walked past him as he pointed to the guest bathroom. She walked into the master bedroom, with Evan following along behind looking a little confused and concerned. Stopping at the foot of his bed, she looked at how neatly everything was tucked in, and the throw pillows were properly in their place. She reached up behind her, grabbing a hold of the zipper to the dress, and pulled it down. The dress fell to the floor, and she turned towards Evan completely naked. Taking two steps, she grabbed Evan's shirt by the flaps that held the buttons, and just pulled. The buttons popped, one after another, going in every direction. Evan stood in shock. Tamra placed her hands on his belly, and started rubbing across its width and up to his chest. Then she grabbed the belt comfortably nestled under his belly, and started undoing it as she dropped to her knees. He couldn't move. As the pants fell to the floor, his long erect penis came shooting out. She took it in her hand, wrapped her lips around it, and grabbed him by the butt taking him all the way in.

"Oh God!" Evan cried, his knees buckling a little. She sucked on his cock for less than ten seconds, before he filled her mouth with cum. It was a different taste than she had ever experienced. It was the taste of complete desire. The unadulterated taste of passionate feelings this man had for her. It was the taste of absolute control and power.

"C'mon, get your pants off!" She climbed on the bed, placing her elbows down on the bed, laying her head down on its side, and poking her butt up in the air. She rocked her hips in a circular motion, as she watched him kick his pants off clumsily. As he started to kneel onto the bed behind her, she lifted her elbows up from the bed, wrapping her hands around his neck so that the curve of his belly fit into the curve of her back. She could feel his cock tickling her back door, so she moved her butt around a little and stuck her tongue in his mouth. She then leaned forward again, rubbing her pleasure against his partially aroused member, and pushed at it, again and again. It wasn't long before he was fully aroused again, and she kept rolling her hips against it. Evan, unsure if he should grab her hips, placed his hands on her back. She reached around, placing his cock inside her, then began rocking back and forward on it, rolling her hips just a bit.

"Oh Shit! Oh Fuck!" Evan kept saying under his breath. He grabbed her hips, pulling on her, as his belly slapped against the top of her buttocks. Within a several minutes, his body was jerking, and he had cum again. "Oh Fuck, Tamra! Oh My God! Damn Woman! I'm sorry."

She turned, laying on her back, and pulled him down on top of her. She ran her hands up his back, while he kissed at her neck, her shoulders, and then down to her breasts. He worked his way down her body till his face rest between her legs. It was not his technique that was arousing to her, because he had none; it was his utter desire to worship her body. She put her hand over his head, pushing down so he could clean up his mess. He wasn't going to make her cum, so she figured she would just make use of his tongue. Sitting up, she pushed on his shoulders to get him to rise to his knees; then moved him to lie on his back. She climbed on top, straddling his waist, feeling a little nudge at her leg. His member showed to be a little eager but spent of energy. Working her way down his belly, she looked into his eyes. Scooting her legs further down, she ran her hands up and down both thighs. She moaned just a little, running her tongue up the inside of his thigh, and then the other, circling with a widened tip in the more sensitive area just below his balls. "Oh Shit! Oh Shit!" He screamed "Oh Fuck Woman!"

His cock hardened once again, and she took him into her mouth. "Oh Shit! Oh My God!"

Climbing on top of him, she reached between her legs grabbing a hold of his member and sticking it in. Rolling her hips in a circular motion, he cried out again and again. She ran her fingers across his chest, and watched his eyes rolling back as he moved his head from one side to the other. He grabbed her hips, and she rocked him faster, and pushed against him harder for several minutes. He cried out again. She thought he was going to cry. There was something so erotic about taking him to a place he had never been before; giving him the pleasure he had only dreamed of; and giving herself in a time of need to someone who will cherish that moment for the rest of his life. His mouth dropped open, and she could see the tension building within him. Too excited to hold it in, he came.

Stepping from the bed, leaving him to lie there alone, she grabbed his shirt off the floor using it to wipe between her legs. She sat back down beside him, running her hand up his leg, "Evan, I need you to keep this between us. I needed you. I needed to feel desired. I needed to feel beautiful. I knew that you would give me all of that. Thank you!" As she picked up her dress, and began to slide it on, she headed for the door.

■■■

9

It was a week of her losing complete control. She could see the desperation of her actions to get a grip on herself. She could see the insanity of the things she was doing, but couldn't stop herself. The fact was that she needed these things to work through the issues that were controlling her. It was her rebellion. She knew how lucky she was to have Richard, and was desperately trying to grasp a hold of what sanity she used to have to salvage that relationship. It appeared that she simply had not been open enough.

She lay on the back patio, alongside the pool, feeling lonely and neglected. Looking around at the furniture, she got up, and went upstairs. Sitting down on Richard's lap, blocking his view of his laptop, she looked at his distracted eyes and kissed him on the lips. "Can you help me move some of the patio furniture?"

"In a minute please, Tamra. I need to get some of this stuff done, so I can pay all your hotel bills. If you're only going to be in there an hour or two, can't you just go to a cheaper hotel?" Richard looked up, and then back to his computer.

She grabbed him by the chin, pulling his eyes back to hers. "I don't use hotel rooms anymore! If you don't come down and help, I understand. I'll just have the landscaping guy help move them." Confidently, she addressed his scolding tone, got up, and went back down to the pool. Looking into the water, she tried to work through the anger that she had no right to have. She knew she had no right to be mad, but she was anyway. Across the yard, the guys tending to the yard were looking at her. When it was obvious that she was looking at them, they slowly parted ways. The one, done with his break, jumped back on the commercial lawnmower, while the other shoveled mulch into the flower beds lining the trees at the eastern edge of the property.

Tamra made her way over to the man with the shovel. As he turned to scoop mulch from the wheel barrow, he stopped to find a beautiful unattended woman standing within a few feet. "Hey!" said Tamra. "I was wondering if I could get a hand moving some things by the pool."

"Sure thing!" said Mitch, tossing the shovel in the wheel barrel. He wasn't very tall, but he was thick. He wore camouflage cargo shorts that were tight against his legs. It was definitely clear that he spent a great amount of time focusing on his body, and ever so glad to show it off. The tight nature of his body, evidence of all the time he had spent focusing on it. To have muscles so plentiful in their size that the veins struggle to find room under the skin, is a testament to the time he had available to spend only on himself.

Tamra looked upon his bulging chest and arms, running her finger down the curve of his bicep across his rough tattoo of a naked woman holding an M-60, wrapped in the ammo belt feeding into it. She then spread her fingers wide till her whole hand was against his skin, and moved her hand up his arm measuring its width with her expanded hand. "Nice tattoo! Where did you get that?"

"Prison!" Mitch rubbed his hand back over his shaved head, a juvenile effort to offer reason for flexing his muscle.

"Nice!" She said, blowing off his misguided bragging rights tone. "Can you take the sunglasses off? I feel like I am talking to a teenager with an ego problem." She turned and walked towards the pool. Lifting her hand just above shoulder level, she raised her index finger and flicked it forward repeatedly to indicate him to follow.

The aggression that he felt was somewhat mixed, anger and sexual tension. Here she was, a beautiful woman in a revealing two piece bathing suit, ordering him around, touching him, and he hadn't been out of prison long enough to even remember how to act properly around a woman. She walked with her shoulders high, and her back slightly arched, making her hips swing just a little bit more. The fabric of the suit slowly moving its way up the crack of her ass, bunching up over the top of her butt cheek. He watched her as she walked, as she slid her fingers across the arch of her butt and under the fabric, and then pulling the fabric out slowly with her finger as the back of her hands moved slowly down the slopes of her cheeks. The fabric would not remain obedient for long, as it worked its way back up where it wanted to be. Mitch could feel his heart pumping, and his saliva begin to dry up, as a nervous energy began to build up inside.

She pointed for him to grab the other side of the table, to move it only a few feet as the umbrella might block her sun; a meaningless task. Through the glass doors, into the basement, she instructed him to follow. Just inside the door a pool table took center stage, with a full bar waiting unattended just behind. To the right of that the wall stopped at the base of the stairs leading up to the rest of the house, and then the guest bedrooms and bathroom completing the layout. She bent over at the hips, her ass in the air, grabbing the small table by the window. "This is too heavy for me; can you help me move it outside?"

He couldn't resist placing his hands on her hips, trying to make it like he was being helpful. "Here, I got that."

As he picked up the table, she placed both hands around the muscles of his bulging arm. "Oh don't hurt yourself. Do you have it?" She then led him outside, showing him where she wanted him to put it. Placing her hand on his arm again, she spread her fingers around the curve of his muscle. "Thank you so much! I was hoping to get some sun today." She turned around, as she tugged on the string of her top just a bit to loosen the knot. "Did you see my lotion inside? I don't see it out here." Placing her hands across the breast cups of her top, the tie string fell loose as she walked back inside. Mitch followed along behind.

Leaning over the pool table, with the top of her thighs pressed against the sides, she held her top to her breasts as she appeared to look for nothing at all. The landscaper, fully aroused now, looking at her ass pushing out slightly, and the curve of her breast sticking out of the side of the loose top, walked up behind her. He grabbed her by the hair, and flipped her around. Pulling her hand away, he grabbed he breast under the suit, and pulled her to his lips. Placing her hand on his chest, as if she objected, she pushed back. "My boyfriend is upstairs!"

"I don't care! I'll kill the fucker if he comes after me!" He pulled her by the hair, down to her knees, unzipping his pants with the other hand. As he pushed his shorts down, he guided her mouth onto his cock. One solid mass of muscle, swollen from years of neglect, suffering years without the touch of a woman, and building years of sexual frustration, filled his loins all at once. Up by the hair he pulled her, throwing her down over the pool table. He pulled at her swimsuit bottoms ripping them off, and just spread her thighs with his hard mass of built up anxiety. She screamed out. He pushed her down on the table, holding her head by the handful of hair held tightly in his grip, pulling up occasionally to look at the face of the woman he was fucking. She screamed as he pounded in an aggressive assault on her pleasure. The pounding on her hips beginning to move the pool table, and scratching the floor. His chest turning red from the heat of his actions, the aggression that he was punishing her with. She screamed. As she tried to catch her breath, she saw the tips of Richard's shoe on the bottom step. The edge of his cheek bone, a lock of hair, and a single eye, peaked around the corner of the stairwell wall. He was watching.

Mitch grabbed her leg, and lifted her by the hair and leg, placing her on her back across the table. He climbed up, pushing her legs into the air, and slid his knees in alongside her hips. Sticking the head of swollen aggression back between her legs, he slammed forward pushing out another scream. He reached across her, grabbing her by the throat, and clenched his grip around her neck, as he slammed his hips into hers again and again. Her cries were choked out, but she could breathe. The muscles in his back showed their tension and strength as he rocked his hips back and forth. His buttocks were hard and round, the skin tight, as he pushed in again and again. He circled with his hips, making her take a deep breath, as his penetration was deep. He circled with his hips, and then he slammed forward. He circled with his hips, and then ramming his hips upward to push the head of his cock up in deep against her vaginal wall. He squeezed her throat, and her cries became erotic panic. All of his built up aggression and all of his muscle being worked out, pounding between her legs. She could see Richard's fingers begin to grip the wall, as he peaked around the edge.

The landscaper pushed up, his grip on her neck tightened. She felt his member striking the limits of her depth. She felt the tingle begin to set in, the numbness take her over. His cock swelling inside her, she felt him pulsate each time he pushed deep. She came. The thick, and throbbing, nature of his member pleasured her where she needed it the most. It was the first time she had cum since James had broke it off. When he was done, she rolled off the table and told him that he could go. Then she locked the door behind him.

Without even bothering to put her suit back on, she walked over to the stairwell, where Richard still stood. She pushed him down gently onto the step, and started pulling at his pants. His cock meeting her lips halfway, she took him deep into her throat, cupping his balls in her gently massaging hand. He leaned back, feeling her passion towards him like he had never felt before. She lifted up, kissing him with deep emotion, and slid down on his member. Her knees on the step, the corner of the step digging into her shins, she didn't care. She rode him till he came. She gave him the passion that he so freely allowed her to explore on her own terms.

■■■

10

On Saturday, Richard took her to a gathering of friends from work, at The Cedar Lake Cellars, in Wright City, Missouri. It was an elegantly laid out winery, with beautiful buildings. The parking lot would get so full with cars that they spilled out into the fields. While Richard tended to his corporate affairs, she wandered about taking in the scenery. They had done a lot with what they had. Wineries tend to position themselves on top of hills where their grapes grow best, and the scenic views give patrons a relaxing atmosphere for sipping wine. This was flat, surrounded by corn fields. But, the lake and the buildings took you to another place. As she walked between the main building and the bathrooms, she stopped dead in her tracks. James, standing with friends, looked at her. He approached, his eyes pleading for her time. She felt the emotion stirring in her gut, emotions that she had fought so hard to suppress and free herself of.

The way he talked to her brought back the memories of the passion she felt when he wooed her with his words. The way he touched her brought back the feeling of the passion between them, and the excitement of their sexual pursuits. He begged her to forgive him for breaking it off. The thought of sharing her was tearing him up, and he couldn't bare it anymore. He pressured her to realize that she didn't really love Richard, and that the passion they had was real. This pursuit of his to use her emotions to control her was giving her anxiety. She had moved on, but she didn't want to hurt him the way he had hurt her.

When his passionate pleas did not seem to work, they turned to threats. It was then that she remembered why letting him go was needed. He was not mature enough to handle anything, and he would never change. She walked away, stepping into the main building where he would have to tone down his threats or attract attention. At the wine sampling bar, he stood behind her smirking. "Tamra, I'll tell Richard everything!"

She looked at James, not saying anything. Over his shoulder, she watched a well dressed, good looking man, step away from his group of male friends, and over to the bar. He was tall, muscular, with short dark hair. Placing her hand on his arm, with James still standing at her side, she squeezed. "Hi. Will you buy me a glass of wine?"

"Sure!" The man smiled, looked at James, and then told the bar tender that he would cover hers too. Stepping past James, she wrapped her arm around the younger man's arm. They talked a bit while they sipped their wine, James finally stepping away but lingering in the backdrop.

"Come with me!" She squeezed the man's arm she stood with, and took him by the hand, leaving James to watch them go. Leading him out into the crowded parking lot, they made their way through the cars to the field where the parking lot had expanded to. Putting her glass of wine on the hood of the Chevrolet Tahoe, she pushed him back against the Ford Expedition behind him. Dropping to her knees, she pulled at his belt. He placed his glass on the hood of the Ford and started pulling at his belt as well. As she pulled at his cock with her lips and tongue, he pulled his shirt up to watch her take it in. Her dress was short, and as it pulled tight against her thighs, the gap between her legs called to him. "Just make me cum!" She stood up, putting her hands against the Tahoe, while he took her from behind. The groups of people that stood around the special event building, where weddings and receptions were primarily held, were too preoccupied to notice the two of them.

He pushed her down further, so her head was pressed against the fender, and she clung to the hood to keep herself up. Bending his knees slightly, he pushed up and in, making her breathing a little more rapid. He pushed up and in, circling the head of his cock deep inside her, making her moans louder and louder. Once he found the spot that brought her to peak pleasure, he pulled at her hips, pushing deep, hitting his mark every time. The louder she moaned the faster and harder he pushed. Her head hitting the fender, as he thrust deep, and his cock throbbed. Gripping her hips tightly, he kept her from falling as her legs became too weak to hold her up. Both of them throbbing and both of them were feeling the gushing between her legs. He leaned against her, on the hood of the Tahoe, while they caught their breath.

Pushing him back against the Ford, she went back down to her knees. Cupping his balls in her hand, she took his cock in her mouth once again. She pulled at its soft nature. She sucked on its soft skin. She moaned as it began to rise again. She sucked harder, and faster, till he was fully erect again. Deep into her throat she took it in, with his hips thrusting up to meet her. He grabbed her hair, thrusting his hips up and down as she sucked hard going in and going out. She stroked its shaft, as she pulled at the head with her lips. He started to tense up, and she could feel him swell. He came. Throbbing and pulsating, filling her mouth with his cum. She swallowed, and then sucked some more to take all he had. He fell back against the truck, breathing a heavy sigh. Standing up, she pulled her skirt down, grabbed her wine, and kissed him on the lips. "Thanks for the wine and the orgasm!"

When she got back to her table, she found Richard away from the group, with James sitting in the chair next to him. "Hey Tamra, I was just telling Richard here how we were old friends, but I hadn't gotten to tell him all the good stuff yet!" He smirked.

"That's okay James!" Tamra smiled back. "You don't control me, but it's obvious that I control you." She straddled Richard, sitting on his lap. Then she kissed him. With her arms resting comfortably on his shoulders, she looked at him with adoring eyes. She popped her chin up, pointing over to a man making his way back through the crowd, with a relaxed look on his face, and a gleaming smile. "You see him. He just bent me over and fucked me in the parking lot. Then I took his cock in my mouth, and blew him. He came so much that I almost choked. Can you taste the fresh cum, Richard? Can you taste the desire?" She kissed him, her lips to his, then her tongue to his. She rose up, putting her tongue deeper into his throat. "I need you to take me out to the parking lot and fuck me, Richard. Let's go!"

"See you around James. No man controls me!" She took Richard by the hand, leaving James alone once again.

The River

All of our dreams seem to be rapidly swept down river without explanation. The river rising suddenly, and without warning, tearing through our lives with devastating force. When it does, we stand along the water's edge watching everything we had worked so hard for, and worked towards building, being taken under by currents that we could not have seen coming. It was this same devastating force that hit her, without notice. Her marriage had ended abruptly, tearing her down to nothing, despite all the warnings. While he had focused on himself, she had to be the one in control of everything else; she was the one that was stable; she brought in the steady income and took care of everything necessary to keep the family together while they worked through those minor bumps all marriages experience. That would all change, when she came home to find him in their bed with another woman. There was that unsettling moment when she walked in, knowing something was wrong. She could hear the moaning echo down the hall. Her heart sank. Her feet felt heavy. She couldn't get herself to move; so, she stood listening to the passion filling her head. It clouded her thinking, and the room began to go dark around her. She could hear herself breathe, as the floor beneath her began to spin, shrinking as her vision blurred; her world was beginning to collapse. Her hand reaching for the wall, to keep herself from falling down. She could hear the bed rocking; the mattress springs squeaking; the headboard beating against the wall. The woman's cries ringing in her ears. Her heart could feel the knife enter, each and every time, keeping rhythm with each thrust of his hips.

    She inched closer to the corner of the wall, not wanting to look, but having to know for certain, and peaked around the corner. The door was open. The woman's legs wrapped around her husband, with her hands gripping his buttocks pulling him in deeper. She cried out each time he went deep; each time he thrust upward. It was a passion that he had never shown her. Falling back against the wall, an old unfilled picture hole digging into the back of Adrienne's head. She just stood there with her eyes closed, listening to them. In too much pain to even muster up anger, she just stood there feeling completely empty and lost. The pain so deep, her tears could not even escape. Her chest felt hollow, just quivering whenever she breathed in, trying to push the tears to the surface.

Their conversation was just so casual, as they got dressed. It was as if they had done this so many times before, there being no doubt that she knew he was married. She heard the door creak, opening just a little wider, and heard their footsteps as they made their way down the hall. The woman was startled at the sight of Adrienne, and then hurried past her out the door. Her husband just stood there for a moment, not looking the least bit bothered at the discovery. "What are you doing home?" He asked, putting his shirt on, not even looking at her. Adrienne looked at him, with new eyes. The betrayal is what hurt the most. It was apparent to her suddenly that the love they once had was no longer there. But, that didn't stop it from hurting. A marriage was never easy, it was something that two people worked through. Sometimes you may not like the person, but there was always that hope that what brought you to them in the first place would come back around. She had been committed to that vow, he had not. She turned without saying a word, and left.

Why did she stand there, and just listen? Why didn't she become irate, charge into the bedroom, and disrupt them in the middle of their passion? She wasn't sure. Something inside her wanted to; wanted to see him in pain for this betrayal. She was brought up proper, to know there were limits to what she was allowed to do or feel. Her responsibility was to her family, and to give the man the room he needed to be the man of the house. All of a sudden, she began to wonder who it was that made these rules she was living by. To her, her mom had shown great strength in holding their family together. But, all along she longed for the freedom that men seemed to have. Times have changed though, and this was not a hardworking man whose primary goal was taking care of his family. She needed time to work this out, because she couldn't think.

The same persuasive confidence that drew other women to him, pulled her back in – though it would never be the same. Her friends told her that she was crazy. Any woman would have left after the first incident, but she stayed to keep her family together. She worked to be more affectionate and went out of her way to accommodate his needs, because the fear of her family falling apart would somehow fall on her as her failure. While things appeared to be stable for quite some time, she could feel his affection become more distant once again. He seemed to intentionally leave the computer logged on. Eventually, she would find herself searching through the social media sites he never signed off of, reading the messages he sent to other women. There seemed to be this tug of war inside her, between the pain and disgust for what he was doing, and this feeling of freedom that he and these other women had – a freedom she so desired. When they had sex, her thoughts were no longer on him, but the fantasies that rolled through her head reading his messages to the others. There were no more feelings for him. There were no more feelings of responsibility to this ceremonial partnership. So, there was no emotional turmoil when she walked in on him again.

Instead, she sat on the couch, down the hall from where the screams, and smacks, bounced off the walls. She heard the slap of his hand across the soft skin of the woman's buttocks; and him scolding her through his teeth "Shut up Whore! Keep that ass up! Keep it up, or I will punish you like never before!" The screams became muffled, fighting to be heard as he pushed the woman's face into the pillows. They were not screams of desperation, but screams of fulfillment. A fulfillment she had never dreamed of achieving. She could see the woman, face down on the bed, head in the pillows. The man's arm, reaching forward, and gripping her by the hair. With each push forward, she saw the woman's hips arch up to meet the man's, and the pleasure each thrust brought visible in her face. Adrienne wanted to feel that free. But, her desires and womanly needs, would again take a backseat to her love, and responsibilities, to her children.

His ego couldn't handle her leaving him, and a long raging battle ensued. The few friends that she had, helped her gather her things while he was at work. Between the attorney mishaps, and his refusal to be reasonable, the divorce drug on for several years. It was her friends that helped her stumble through, as her life turned from controlled and structured, to clumsy and out of control. Through the strain of tedious fights, she would eventually win custody of the kids. It wasn't that he didn't love them, but he was not a care taker, and he would not give them what they needed to feel loved every moment of every day. Through the divorce, all her attention was focused on making the kids feel as if nothing had really changed. She padded that nest like a mother preparing for the worst of winters. As the divorce had neared an end, she was feeling overwhelmed, but couldn't miss out on her bestie Karen's birthday party at Cedar Lake

Cellar's, in Wright City, MO. It was a truly romantic, and relaxing, environment for any gathering. It was the weekend after Fourth of July, so they would have fireworks to bring the evening to one glorious end.

This gathering of women, to lift up the spirits of another woman, always benefited them all. There was no one better than friends. The simple laughter these women offered her, lifted more weight off of her shoulders than any man could ever think to do. Not that a man wasn't needed. The more wine they drank, the more they laughed. The more wine they drank, the less they gossiped – instead, their comments went from criticism to what they would have done. The more wine they drank, the less they cared what anyone thought. While busy having a little too much fun, they were attracting everyone's attention. Hank, an old schoolmate of Karen and Adrianne's, saw them and approached the group. His smile gleaming from ear to ear. He hadn't seemed to age a bit, only looking better with age. Adrienne could feel her guard letting down, as his charm took hold. They talked and joked, taking her back to a time when she was a little more carefree and happy. Abandoning his friends, he joined the group for the extra attention offered by a handful of upbeat, attentive, women clinging to the one single man they could flirt with. The spirit of the laughter, and the company of good friends, putting everyone at ease.

It wasn't long before Adrienne found herself smiling again and enjoying this man's company. He convinced her to dance with him, the live band playing music from a time when she had no troubles, and she had nothing but fond memories. She felt young again. When the music slowed, and the songs took that journey to times of intimacy and passion long in the past, she could feel the emotion of her girlish dreams revived. The weight of her troubles lifted as he took her into his arms. His arm around her waist, she felt her tension ease. The closeness of his body to hers, she could feel his warmth and strength. Her body remembered that feeling of security; that feeling of longing; that feeling that everything was going to be alright. She could feel the air escape her chest; the imprisoned desire held within her beginning to surface; and she finally allowed herself to just feel like a beautiful woman once again. When the song ended, their embrace did not. She didn't pull away, nor did she want the feeling of being held to end. Taking her chin with his hand, he ran his thumb gently across her lips, looking into her eyes. She didn't move. He held her chin, putting his lips to hers. The softness of his lips, and the caress of his tongue to hers, making her body weightless like she didn't need to breathe at all. A sudden fear of being out of control creeped in, and she placed her hand on his chest. "I'm sorry! I can't!" She pushed him away, covering part of her face while she attempted to focus and regain control. She walked away.

Rejoining the group, Hank sat next to her, not relenting on his advances. Placing his hand on her leg from time to time. The conversation eventually putting her at ease again before she could put her walls back up. As much as she tried to keep her feelings at a distance, she did not push his advances away. Part of her needed this man's attention; this man's affection; this man's advances; and how much she needed to be desired again. She just could not give herself permission, for fear of being hurt. But, even after her friends had started to disappear, she remained. When two of her friends were leaving to go to another party, he encouraged her to join them – but she remained. She stayed with him, because deep down she needed, and was searching for, the permission to be free - permission she just couldn't give herself. They sat at the edge of the lake, watching the fireworks light up the night sky. There could not be anything more romantic, than fireworks on a clear night, with a full moon lingering in the distance. His hand stroking her thigh, making its way up and down along her smooth skin, sliding easily between the thighs from time to time. She did not avoid his advances. They talked long into the evening, not even realizing that most everyone had already left. When Hank had excused himself to use the restroom, he saw that there was no one else around. On his walk back, there was the occasional employee clearing tables off in the distance. They had stayed after closing, and didn't know it.

At the edge the lake, where she still sat in the wooden lounger, she looked up as he stepped around, standing before her. He leaned forward, pushing her crossed legs apart, placing one hand on her thigh, and grabbing her chin with the other. His lips to hers, he slid his hand deep between her legs, grabbing her pleasure. Startled, she gasped, looking around to see if there was anyone there. "Don't worry, I see them." He said. He grabbed her by the back of the hair, pulling her head back as his lips, and his tongue, moved from her lips to her neck. He could hear the air escape her lungs, and he pushed in deeper between her legs to awaken what she had denied herself for so long. Through muffled moans, she tried to breathe. With his lips to hers, he pulled her top down exposing her breast, taking it into his mouth. Her breathing became more rapid, and he began to move the hand between her legs with purposeful motion. Then the other breast, and again to her lips. He moved his lips, his tongue, and his teeth across her neck, and chest, to leave nothing untouched. It had been so long, and the passion came so quick and forceful, that it wasn't long before she couldn't catch her breath. He pulled at her shorts, tugging the zipper all the way down. But she stopped him, looking over towards the employees clearing tables. Not fighting, he moved his hand back between her legs. She fully surrendered, her eyes remaining closed as she relinquished control to him. Her back arched, he could feel her thighs pushing together, and her breathing begin to stop – then quiver. When she came, her thoughts were lost to some distant cloud, her eyes closed, not hearing his pants unzip.

    The hair on her neck felt numb as his hand slid around behind her neck, grabbing her by the hair once again, then pulling her forward. She felt the head of his cock part her lips, pushing its way in, parting her teeth without a fight. He stood, looking over the empty chairs that littered the grass around the lake, pushing his cock deep into her throat. The ridges of his erection pressing down on her tongue along the way; pushing her jaws open. He pulled her up, pushing her forward onto the back of the chair, yanking down on her shorts. She couldn't stop him, both hands pinned against the back of the chair.

She started to cry out, but he covered her mouth with his hand. "Shhhhhh!". With his hand cupped around her mouth, he massaged her ear with his lips and tongue. The other hand sliding down between her legs. He eased his fingers in, feeling the tight nature of her neglected pleasure. There was no stopping him now. She didn't care. The motion of his fingers putting her body at ease, and putting her body in the motion it wanted the fingers to move. Before she was even ready, she felt his fingers slide out, and what seemed like something enormous to her, slide in. It had been too long, and she had forgot the feeling of a man being inside. With his hands moving to her hips, he pushed himself in deeper; pushing the air from her body. There was nothing to truly describe the feeling to her. Each stroke; each thrust; each upward motion; and each circling of his hips taking her to another place. Her eyes struggling to stay open, letting her concerns drop away. To the right, she saw a young man clearing the table within ear shot, and clear view. She watched another waitress walking from the main building across to the open event area to the north, without looking over at them. She no longer cared. He grabbed her shoulders, pulling on her, as he slammed his hips against her. She came again. She could feel him swell, his passion becoming more aggressive and enlarged. Then the throbbing of his member within her, giving her new sensation.

When they had dressed themselves, he walked her to her car. He gave her one last kiss, smacking her ass as he walked away. There was no "hey baby" or "I'll call you tomorrow." He just left. It would be weeks before she heard from him again. He had tracked her down through friends, and they met up at Ethyl's Barbeque in O'Fallon. They talked a little, and had a few drinks. At the end of the evening, he walked her to her car. They kissed, but she was keeping it more formal, and guarded, this time. She started her car, and turned to look up at him, only to find his cock in her face. He gripped her by the hair, pulling her down onto him. She obeyed. When he came, he leaned over, and gave her a kiss good night. Then he turned and walked away. There were several more encounters, and she let them happen. To release control, to someone else, gave her a little freedom. But it wouldn't last long. She could feel her kids pain, as they watched their father bounce from one relationship to another – only wanting their family to be back to what it was, which, with their skewed memory, was much better than it had actually been. She couldn't, and wouldn't, do that to her children. She swore off men, and any relationships, till they were out of the house. That day would come quicker than she ever thought.

It was the one and only Fast Eddie's Bon Air, to start her evening out. Adrienne's friends were taking her out to melt the cold shoulders that were beginning to isolate her from the rest of the world. To take her to a place to escape. The legendary dive bar, originally owned by Anheuser Bush itself. Where else do you go but Fast Eddie's, when you are anywhere near Alton, Illinois? The ultimate beer and food bar near the river. On the weekends, you are lucky just to find standing room - with shrimp and bratwurst in one hand, and beer in the other. The atmosphere was gearing her up to party. She was ready!

Her friends had gathered together, for a girl's night out. They had to push her to pull her out of her routine; to get her out of her hermit sanctuary; to bring her to life; to remind her what it was to live. This burden she had been carrying far too long, and it had become time for her to unload. Everything that was being bottled up inside her was pushing her deeper into a solitude, and she was losing herself in the process. Adrienne sat at the table, beginning to feel a little more carefree after several glasses of beer, or in reality she had just begun to no longer feel like her problems were controlling her.

She joked with her friends that what she needed was a ship full of lonely sailors to park their ship in her port. It wasn't very often that she got out; now that she was free of the children she dedicated her life to, and was able to let herself feel free to take care of only her needs. She had simply reached a point in her life where she was done playing by the rules: always being the good girl, a good woman, and a good wife. It was like suddenly wanting to feel what it was like to be the bad girl and go to jail, for once! After one too many drinks, she began grabbing the butts of men she thought were cute, as they walked by. The men didn't mind, but her friends were embarrassed. It was too crowded for anyone to really know who touched whose butt. She was feeling ornery, and the crowd of drunken men was making her feel a little more free and wild. She just needed to get laid. When her friends were talking about going elsewhere, she was left out of the conversation. She had become the drunken friend that would just be drug along with the group. Before she could finish the beer in her hand, friends had grabbed each of her arms as they moved her through the crowd. She was able to stop them, to grab a butt cheek or two, of men who she was sure she was destined to be with - her friends didn't seem to think so. Out the door and in the mom van she was pushed. They were off.

The Argosy Casino was only a few minutes away. She wanted to hang with her friends, but gambling was not what was on her mind. As her group of friends drug her down the entrance ramp, talking about what a blast this girl's night out was, she envisioned being transported into another world - and she was. She was transported into what felt like the cheesiest old person casino she could imagine. The atmosphere was drab, and uninspiring. It made her feel like she had just walked into a cheap rental house version of Las Vegas. They were all so drunk it didn't really matter, but she just couldn't get into the mood to gamble. She ordered some nachos from the cheesy café, and sat down at the cheesy sports bar with its different sports channels on. The only men at the bar, were old enough to be her father, or were there because it was their best hope at picking up a chic at a bar. Looking at her nachos, which looked more like some chips covered with a bad salad, she just flipped them off the bar, onto the cooler below, while the bartender looked on. "Those aren't nachos!"

The bar tender nodded as she cleaned up the mess. "I know honey! I'm not sure what you call those!" Adrienne guzzled down her beer, throwing an apology tip down on the bar.

Walking over to one friend after another, she pulled at them, trying to get them to take her back to Fast Eddies Bon Air. One after another blew her off, pulling their slot machine handles down and screaming for a win. She told them that she was walking back to Fast Eddies, and they seemed to ignore her. So, when they did go to leave, they would be consumed with worry when they couldn't find her, or worry that in her flirtatious state that she would just leave with any guy. But, she was too drunk to care what they would think later, and she just wanted to get back to the crowd of fertile men under the age of seventy. She exited the boat ramp, and looked around. To her right, she could see the triangular peaks of the bridge leading into Missouri. She knew Fast Eddies was to the east of that, so made her way right down the middle of the drive lane with an Argosy Shuttle Bus following patiently behind because it had no way around her.

About halfway through the parking lot of the Alton Amphitheater, just east of the Argosy, she got tired of walking and just stepped over to the painted black metal fence that overlooked the river. Tucking herself in a corner of the fence, behind some small trees, she leaned on the fence looking out upon the water. It was beautiful, just to see the reflection of the moon on the water, and watch it become distorted in the ripples swirling along the top. She watched as a barge made its way down river, pointing towards where she stood, and then started to angle its nose out as it drifted a bit towards shore. She could see the crew starting to scramble, readying tie down ropes. She laughed at herself, as she thought about her much-needed sailors pulling into her port. The wall, below the railing she leaned on, dropped straight down into the river below, set up with tie downs for the large boats used on the River Cruises, and a ramp to offload passengers. The boat edged closer, and she realized that it was actually going to dock in front of her. She could see the crew members, who moved swiftly from one barge to the next, visibly sweating, and their hardened bodies glistening in the moon's light. The curves of their muscles lightly shadowed in the valleys where the muscles meet and the moon failed to penetrate. With only one rope hooked onto the wall, she watched two crew members make their way up the ramp, and up and over the padlocked fence. She could hear the pilot screaming for them to hurry up. At a rapid walk, breaking into the occasional jog, the two men made their way towards the casino. The location was not exactly authorized for the docking of a barge, but they didn't seem to care. The crew members would return half dragging the Captain, flipping him over the fence one drunken leg at a time, and loading him on the boat. An unruly crew needed an unruly Captain to keep them in line. Just watching the men with their reckless disregard for the rules, and the roughneck nature of how they treated each other, she could feel their bad nature pulling at her. Their movements crossing from one railing to the next, jumping from barge to barge, and the strength it must take to throw the lines and equipment they tossed around like feathered pillows, just pulled at her desires like controlling strings. A little intoxicated, maybe more than a little, but most of what was driving her was not the absence of inhibition from drinking – it was simply her need to explore her desires, and to feel that out of control passion she had once felt. The memories of the man who took her at the winery were coming back. The control he had taken then, and several times after. She was dripping wet, and there was a relentless throbbing between her legs.

As the crew stepped out of view, she hopped the fence, made her way down the ramp, stepped onto the deck, moving aft towards the stern. She committed herself to a mischief she had long wanted, but never had the courage to commit. Even if it did not turn out as she had dreamed, it was still worth the feeling of the freedom and power that it gave her. She sat down in the curled-up tow ropes on the starboard side of the stern, leaned back and closed her eyes. She just wanted to live through her fantasy in her mind while sitting on deck. It would appear that she was more intoxicated than she thought, and her eyes were closed longer than she thought. When she opened those eyes of hers, she looked up at the stars. The seven sisters, of the Taurus constellation, were clear as day; but it was also moving. Lifting up, she saw the head of grey hair lowering between her legs. She put the soles of her feet against the shoulders of the man, and pushed back.

As he was rolling up the rope on the port side that had been tied up to the wall, he had looked over to find her laying there with her eyes closed. "Hey there little lady, I was just trying to make sure you were all right!" Skip reached up, placing his hands on the inside of her knees, he smiled, pushing her legs apart - glancing down again as he did. "You just seem a little drunk there lady. Let me help you." He looked down between her legs, sliding one hand down her thigh, as he extended his other hand to help her up. Skip, a nickname that stuck with him all his life, was a somewhat attractive older man, although kind of brutish and grungy, with his long hair pulled back in a ponytail, the muscular tone of his face and neck stood out. There was a firm, strong, and aggressive look about him. His clothes in tatters, hanging on his abused body; abused from years of hard labor, the careless indestructible thinking of male youth, and willingness to push on through whatever pain he was facing. He was not her type, but it was arousing to her in a roughneck sort of way; in a slumming it sort of way, and he was still a good looking man. The desire in his eyes made her feel enormously sexy, very beautiful, and the thought of him just taking her on that deck was arousing her. She laid her head back down on the ropes, looking up at the stars. The extended helping hand that he offered made its way back onto her thigh. She could feel how excited he was getting in the pausing nature of his touch. His hands were thick, rough and calloused, from years of hard labor. The sharp edges of his calloused fingertips, where he had bit off the skin along with his nails, scratched at her sensitive skin as he moved them up her inner thighs.

She could hear his breathing getting heavier as he savored the feel of her thighs. This was not some meaningless touch to him, to quickly satisfy his needs and be done. He was treasuring the feel of her skin, the softness of her thighs, the smell of her skin, and having the pleasure of her beauty. She closed her eyes, as she felt his lips begin to caress her thigh. He was covering every inch of her leg with his lips, not wanting to miss one spot. Breathing her in deep, she could hear the adrenaline of his racing heart interrupt his breath in waves. The heat of his breath, his excitement trapped under her dress, and between her thighs, as he exhaled. His excitement alone made her wet. With his hands on her hips, he put his lips between her thighs and began to express his desire with his lips and tongue, like it was the very reason he existed. This was just pure lust. Her beauty had pulled at him, and he had to have her, possess her, care for her, but the fact she lay willingly, even if drunk, just overruled any degree of restraint that he might have had. There was no hesitation in anything he did, reminding her how desirable she really was.

Unconvincingly, she played the part of the passed-out victim, lasting only a little bit, and slowly fading the longer he spent exploring her passion with his lips and tongue. She could not help but place her hand on the back of his head, running her fingers back till they reached the string that pulled it all together. She grabbed his pony tail, and moved his lips and tongue where they needed to be the most. The repeated torture of his misadventures, missing the mark, was too much for her to handle. Pushing him in deep, he seemed to get more excited. His hand sliding up her dress, he pushed his fingers underneath her bra, and squeezed the breast that he took in his hand. Continuing upon his guided task, he felt her thighs begin to squeeze the sides of his face. He pushed his fingers up inside her to relieve the pressure, as the throbbing began to set in. Continuing to arouse the nerves, he made her back arch up, pushing her tummy towards the sky, as she pushed his face further down. Squeezing his head between her thighs, she didn't care about him, only what he could do. She came. He gripped her breast with the same intensity that her thighs squeezed the sides of his head.

Pulling at the rope that tied his pants around his waist, his baggy pants fell to the ground. The head of his erection shining in the moonlight, he grabbed her by the legs and shoved himself between them. His excitement was pounding. His passion was forceful. His desire was rough. The ropes dug into her back, as he pushed himself in deep. His grunting and breathing as rough as his thrusts were upon her. She was wet just from the feel of his aggression, the pounding strokes of his member inside her, and the feel of his hips slamming into hers. She watched as the constellations rolled by, one after another, their glimmering light shaking a bit at each rocking of his hips. His breathing heavy, but his passion was not showing signs of losing ground. The rough and weather chapped lips nipped at her neck, as he pushed in deep. She felt his breathing change, becoming more rapid, his desire becoming more pronounced, and his passion swelling even more. He thrust in harder, and faster, the rope digging hard into her back. Then his forehead came to rest on her shoulder, as the pumping of his hips slowed. His head lifting up, she could hear the waves of breath as he came. When he was done, he pulled up his pants and retied his rope.

He wasn't done with her yet. Looking around, he pulled her up, leaned forward, and threw her over his shoulder. Making his way around the Texas Deck, to sneak her into the bulk head where the crews' quarters were, he made his way down the alley way to his room. The pilot had taken his position at the helm, and since their crew was running short, they only had the Lead Hand and two Deckhands on watch. The Lead was Butch, a large muscular man, shaved head, and goatee. He was rough, probably spent as much time in prison as he did on the outside. For the most part, he had achieved his position simply through brute strength. No one gave him any lip, so he was always able to get the job done. If they were shorthanded, his crew always made do. He had the two Mexicans that barely spoke English working underneath him, but they were able to accomplish anything that needed done without complaint.

When he went down to wake the other crew before the break of dawn, so they could scarf their breakfast down before watch, he heard noises coming from behind Skip's door. Skip had slept very little, exploring Adrienne's body while he had the opportunity, showering her body with his kisses from head to toe, and tasting her skin from one end of her beautiful body to the next. Hurriedly, he threw his pants and shirt on, when the knock came. He opened the door a crack, trying to squeeze out without opening the door too much. But, Butch was taller than he was, and there was no blocking his view. When Butch saw the lump under the sheets, he pushed the door open, ripping the handle from Skip's grip. "What do we have here?" Butch looked at Skip.

"I found her lying on deck last night, drunk. I figured I'd let her sleep it off, and we could drop her off at the next port. C'mon, Butch. Don't tell the Captain." Skip pleaded.

"Go get your grub, and get on deck." Butch waved him off. As Skip made his way down the alley way, Butch looked at the curves of her body underneath the sheet. Her right hip was slightly exposed, the sheet curving over her butt cheek, and then sloping back down before edging across her back. Her naked shoulder completely exposed, with the curve of her breast visible underneath her arm as the arm curved up under the pillow her head lay on. He could see her nipple in the shadows of the sheets, perky and waiting. Lifting up on her elbows slightly, she turned and looked at him, then laid her head back down facing the back wall. She heard the door close, but could still hear movement. Unsure if it was outside or in, she turned to look again, finding the large muscular man now half undressed with his pants on the ground. The shadows moving across his broad chest, as light flickered in from the small portal window in the room. The hair on his chest adding darkness to his skin, the curves of his chest muscles taking her breath away, making her feel somewhat frightened and powerless. Before she could move, he had yanked the sheet off of her, and pinned her face down on the mattress. His member pressed hard into her buttocks. With his hand gripped tightly around her mouth, he put his lips to her ear. She felt his breath on her ear. "You know you want it! You scream and I will snap your neck!"

With his chest against her back holding her down, and his hand clenching her mouth tight, he reached down grabbing his cock, and pushing it between her tensed up thighs. She didn't invite this man in, but he was taking her regardless. She felt so helpless. A man she hadn't even met, forcing his way into the room, and taking her against her will. She could feel his aggression. She could feel his strength. She could feel the power and control he had over her. This was jailhouse aggression pumping through his hips. He spread her. He moved her skin. He split her legs. The pain absorbed by the erotic feeling. The weight of his body and tight grip making her juices flow. The force of his cock up inside her brought another level of feeling deeply desired. He gripped her tight. He ripped her right. He pushed. He rammed her with all the built-up aggression he had inside. She arched her buttocks up to meet his thrust, getting him in deeper. Biting down on her neck, he pushed in deep and held the thickness up in her. She could feel the pressure against her walls.

He pumped, and the bed rocked. He pumped, and the bed creaked. He pumped, and she screamed. She bit his finger in defiance, and he squeezed her face harder. She bit down more, and he grabbed her hair, pushed himself up, and slapped the ass he was pushing against with an open hand. The smacking sound could be heard several hallways away. She screamed through the sheets as he continued shoving her head into the mattress. He pumped, and the bed rocked. He pumped, and the bed creaked. He pumped, and she screamed. She bit his fingers again, and his fingers dug into her face, squeezing. She screamed as he hammered his way in; as he hammered his way through; as he hammered her like she had never been fucked before. Her ass lifting up, feeling the numbness from his pounding, she pushed back against him. His muscle, and the undeniable power of his strength, controlled her every move. Keeping her legs between his, it kept her pelvic muscles tight against his member. He pushed.

As his thrusts moved her across the bed sheets, her head began to hit the wall. She broke one of her arms free from his grip, and pushed her hand against the wall to hold her back. Her back muscles tensed up, and she arched her buttocks up to meet the hard slamming of his thrusting hips. She could feel his rage. She could feel his strength. She could feel the force of his aggression upon her. His member began to swell and throb, and his motion would slow as he came deep within her.

He climbed off her, grabbed a towel off the shelf on the wall, and tossed it onto the back of her head. "Here's a towel. Go clean yourself up. The shower room is across the hall." As he zipped up his pants, he closed the door behind him.

■■■

Adrienne, pulled the towel off her head, rolled out of bed, and threw it around her. She was kind of in a daze, feeling a little empty, but feeling the arousing nature of what was playing out. It made her wet. She stepped through the door, a shared shower room across the hall with six showerheads in an open tiled corner of the room. To her left were the sinks, shelves and some general bathroom accommodations. Adrienne tossed her towel on the bench at the edge of the shower, and then tripped over the room divider a she stepped in. She didn't seem to pay much attention to the two Mexicans standing there, taking a shower. Tilting her head back, she stood under the water and let it cover her body. The warmth coating her felt good, massaging her body on its way down to her feet. The Mexicans just looked on, not as if they were going to leave any time soon. They were young men, who've been on the boat without a woman for weeks. She reached over to the man, Jose, who stood nearest to her, and took the bar of soap out of his hand. A bit startled, he watched as she circled the bar of soap around her breast, and then the other. The soap lathered up as she circled around her nipple, underneath the breast, and then back around again. As the bar left a trail of soap heading down between her legs, Jose became aroused. Adrienne looked down at his erection, and then looked up into his eyes - as if seeing him for the first time.

He stepped forward, pressing her back against the wall, with the water from the shower now rolling down his back. Grabbing her by the chin, he cocked his head to the side, and looked to her mouth, her neck, and then her breasts. He took a breast into his hand, and then into his mouth. She wrapped her fingers around his manhood, stroking it gently, as she felt him pull at her nipple, and dropped the bar of soap to the floor. Her hands flat against the wall, and her shoulders pressed back, she pushed her breasts up for him to take more. He pulled her in by the waist, tight against his body with his teeth digging into her breast. Releasing her breast, he grabbed her by the hair, and turned her around. Pulling at her hips, she could feel his member pushing between her butt cheeks. With the pressure, he applied on her shoulder, he pushed her down. Reaching down, he grabbed a hold of his member pushing the head between her lips. He rolled the tip around, softening the expectation anxiety, preparing her body for the intrusion, and awakening her arousal. Grabbing her by the shoulder with one hand, and her hip with the other, he eased his erect nature between her thighs. She gasped. Once fully in, he pulled out slowly, then pushed in again, pulled out slowly to just push in once again.

As the pace of Jose's thrust picked up with the slamming of his hips against hers, Pablo made his way over, reaching underneath to grab a breast. With the other hand he grabbed her by the hair, steering her away from the wall. His manhood, hard and throbbing, pressed against her lips. He pushed it between them, parting her teeth as he pulled back on her hair. The head of his swollen cock, pushing her tongue down as it made its way to the back of her throat. He pushed a little harder, expanding her throat, and cutting off her air. Pablo was too large for her to take him all the way into her throat, but he tried; pulling at her hair, and pushing with his hips. Then out again. Her hands on his thighs, she would push back so she could breathe. The effort was fruitless, with Pablo pulling on her hair, and Jose slamming into her hips from behind, the penetration on both ends was going as deep as it could. Their seven plus inches of Mexican meat tenderized her body, thrusting themselves upon her, and pounding her on both ends. She could feel herself weaken, and her body feeling light, as Jose pushed in deep, pushed in hard, and pushed in fast. Pablo shoved his cock into her open mouth, as she faded off into the wave of tingling rolling through her body. She didn't want to move. Her knees started to give way to the weight of her body.

Jose kept pushing, thrusting, and sliding himself in and out rapidly, down and then thrusting up again, as her knees buckled and she went down to the floor. He pressed down on the middle of her back, slowing his push, leaning forward so his thrusts were downward and pushing against the wall of her uterus. She gasped. Pablo lowered himself to the floor in front of Adrienne, and pulled her by the hair back onto his cock. She tried to please him, but the euphoric cloud that was consuming her body made it difficult for her to do anything. Her head lowered to the floor as she came, the orgasm taking her strength. Pablo again pulling her up by the hair, placing the head of his cock in her mouth, while she felt Jose throbbing, pumping cum deep within her. When he pulled out, Pablo laid back pulling her on top of him. Leading her by the hair, he ran her mouth, and tongue, the length of his cock, up to his abdomen. The muscles rippled from years of hard labor on the boat, now shining under the water that rained down upon them. Reaching down between her legs, she slid down onto his cock, slowly, spreading her just a bit more. She could feel its girth. She could feel the ridges of its shaft. She gripped his chest muscles squeezing, as he pushed upwards.

Jose stepped around in front, grabbing her by the hair, his cock still half erect. He placed it in her mouth, its softened nature sliding back on her tongue to her throat. He gripped her hair pushing his pelvis against her face. His directions were in Spanish, but she probably would not have heard them anyway. The thick shaft between her legs thrusting upward, spreading her lips at each push, and the large half erect cock rolling on her tongue and filling her mouth, were distraction enough. He held his cock in her throat, and then slowly pulled out. He barked at her in Spanish again. She began sucking hard, feeling him start to thicken slightly. Harder she sucked. Harder Jose gripped her hair and pulled her in. Harder Pablo slammed upward. She was feeling somewhat numb, euphoric, or weak, but she wasn't sure which. Jose pulled at her hair, shoving his cock deep into her throat. Pablo pulling at her hips, jamming his rock hard member up inside her. She was feeling the pounding at both ends, an erotic numb.

Digging her fingers into Pablo's chest, he pushed harder and faster. Jose's cock began to fill her mouth, and spread her jaws, as he began to get hard once again.

Jose stepped over to the bathroom sink, and grabbed the pump of lubricant off the sink. A water based lubricant, since oil based lubricants were hard to wash away making their hands slippery while working on deck. He stepped back over, slapping the lubricant on his hand; he coated his member, and pushed her down onto Pablo's chest. Feeling the muscles of both men's bodies pressing against her body, she could feel the ripples when their bodies tensed. The hard grip of their calloused hands guided her, moved her, and pressured her. She could feel the head of his member slowly sliding between her butt cheeks, with his chin digging into her shoulder. He smiled at her, rattling off words she couldn't understand. She felt him enter her back door, spreading her hips. Her back muscles tensed up as she felt him slowly guiding it in. The two cocks rubbing against each other through the thin wall of skin separating the chambers. When the initial discomfort had passed, perhaps because she was so turned on, she began to feel the motion of both cocks grinding on her G-spot and vibrating her clit, making the feeling indescribable. It was a feeling like she had never felt before. She had tried anal before, but never like this. With her eyes closed she began to see stars shooting across the dark recesses of her mind. She was lost in the deep feeling of the motion, and the way her body was tingling.

The bodies of the two men pressed against her, one on top, and one underneath. One, forcing her down on the other, a bed of tight skin and hardened muscle. So much power on top, and so much power below. The feel of their muscles, up inside her and out. The motion of their selfish pleasure, forced upon her. She could feel the pressure each time Jose tensed up his buttocks, and his member pressed deeper. She felt the two cocks rubbing, visualizing it in her mind, having both holes filled. She felt the darkness of pleasure, alone and relaxing. She felt the tingle rolling through her body, and her body weakening. A shutter ripple through all her nerve endings, making it feel like all the blood she had was pulled down to her hips. Her thoughts drained with the blood, her mind in a soft empty cloud. The heat from their bodies on hers, the water channeled down the sculpted lines of muscles of the three bodies in motion. She couldn't speak. She couldn't cry out. Her body was shaking, shuttering, going numb, and the orgasm simply earth shattering. Her mind feeling blown, unable to breath, she just collapsed onto Pablo's chest gripping him. Jose came, picked up the bar of soap, and rinsed off. Pablo continued, gripping her hips, and rocking her up and down. She just held on, and came again. When finished, he moved her off him, leaving her on the floor of the shower, and the warm water caressing her body.

■■

It didn't seem like she was laying there for that long, still feeling the pleasure of the pressure that had been between her legs. Jamal, a large Jamaican deckhand, stepped into the room, a towel wrapped around his waist. He looked at the naked woman lying on the floor, as he tossed his towel and shower kit on the bench. "Hey! What you doing here lady, eh?"

She looked up to find this large dark skinned black man approaching her. His body toned and massive, arms and legs bulging with strength, and his member hanging large between his legs. She couldn't take her eyes off of it. Her focus on his member did not go unnoticed, and he would never leave a woman wanting. He waved his fingers for her to sit up, placed his fingers under her chin, and his large thumb in her mouth. She looked at his member, while feeling his thumb pressing down on her tongue, and then pushing against her lips. With his other hand, and took his cock in his hand and pushed it between her lips. The size of his member, at this soft stage, filled her mouth. Its warmth teased her taste buds. Its soft girth pushed at her cheeks. She stroked, and pulled at it with her mouth as she felt it grow. It pushed her jaws apart, and she opened wider to keep her teeth from digging in. Before long, she could only fit the tip in her mouth, and she pulled at the shaft of his cock which was the size of her own forearm.

The thought of its size filling her mouth made her wet, dripping wet. She stroked it with both her hands, trying to stretch her mouth around it and take it deeper. She could feel the ridges of his shaft, and the pulse of the protruding veins, as she ran her tongue up its length.

Picking up the lubricant that still lay on the floor; he slapped some on his member. He grabbed her underneath the arms, lifting her up, pushing her against the far wall. Taking his right hand, he placed two fingers up between her legs, and then slid in a third. With his forearm against her neck, he began sucking on her breasts. His thick fingers pushing at her walls, spreading her vulva, and making her gasp for air. He pushed in a fourth, and she cried out. Grabbing her by the throat, he lifted her up against the wall; wrapping her legs slightly around his arms as he did. Her hands felt so tiny gripping the arm that held her up, not being able to reach his shoulders to push up. All she could do was hang on. Gripping the shaft of his enlarged member, pulling his fingers out from inside her, and he held it straight up to slide her on. Its head almost larger than the gap between her legs. The tip pressed against her lips, pushed against her vulva. She dug her heels into the curve of his buttocks to slow her descent, as the head of his cock spread her legs. The pressure of its soft strength against her muscles, and the stretching of her passion, made her wet. The initial discomfort passed, as she slid down on it slowly. Smacking his shoulders, she cried out. The stretching felt so good, but with a little bit of pain. The feeling of his head filling her up, pushing against her vaginal walls, she pulled on his dread locks with one hand while beating on his shoulder with the other as he banged his cock off her cervix. She felt taken. She felt like he was tearing her in half. It felt so good, the thought just made her wet. The heat from the friction, as he pushed it up in her; then out, and then in again, numbed her senses. She couldn't take him all the way in, but it was his thickness that made her forget where she was. The pushing against her insides brought about new sensations. She wrapped her arms around his neck, gripping his hair in her hand. Her head against his, she just held on for the ride with her eyes closed and her mind in a different place.

She could feel the pressure against her walls. She could feel each thrust ripple through her body. With her eyes closed, she could see waves in her darkness moving with the upward rocking of his cock. Her body was weightless and heavy at the same time. All her senses were numb, her nerves overloaded with feeling, and just the feeling of being filled up by his large cock on her mind. She felt his shaft harden a little more, spreading her just a little bit more, and his head swelled pushing at her internal walls. He lifted her off, lowering her to the ground. Placing the head of his cock in her mouth, he held the back of her head, and stroked his member. Grabbing her hair, he tilted her head back slightly, as cum shot out covering her face. Her face completely covered in white, with streams rolling down, he placed the head back between her lips releasing the rest into her mouth. She ran her tongue around the head of his cock, licking off what was left. Then he stepped away to take his shower, leaving her on the floor. She just sat on the floor, even after Jamal had finished showering and left, feeling the numbness between her legs.

Butch stepped into the shower a bit later, turning the water off. He tossed a towel at Adrienne. "C'mon, it's time to go! The Captain is going to pull over at the next docking area and let you off. So, let's get you dressed."

As the barge eased its way up alongside the wall, an area normally used for loading product such as grain into the box barges, Butch readied her at the edge to disembark. When the tug brushed the large rubber bumpers, Butch helped with a shove, encouraging her to jump across the gap between the boat and wall. She stumbled a little, getting her feet underneath her, and turned to watch the crew standing on deck as they started to pull away. They simply stood looking at her, like they were losing something; like they were leaving something behind. There was a feeling of anonymity in being left there alone, as if she had been given the chance to live that fantasy with no remorse.

Poems

The Keys of Love

Oh how they long for the days of chivalry so long in the past.

Those times where the words "love you forever' seemed to last.

A system of rights and rules, causing traditional romance to crumble.

Decades of lawsuits and offenses making the male suitor stumble.

All the ceremony gone, flowers wilting in the stores all alone.

The father's permission no longer needed, for the girls are all grown.

Now distance becomes the key to finding love without offense.

Awkward ceremony is this, the pressing of the right key.

Dating online, your loneliness and pain for the world to see.

So many will get hurt in this world so absent of romantic pursuit.

Before there is pain, and they get hurt, they unplug so the plea is mute.

Somewhere in that exchange the romance got lost.

In the crowded waves of data, their signals got crossed.

They move on so quickly, to the next romance.

Every time they hit a key, giving love another chance.

Surrender (The Ballerina)

Cast me gently into the morning air.

I give you my problems I can no longer bear.

Take them unto your shoulders so strong.

I place all my trust in you to do no wrong.

All of my weaknesses I expose to you.

Just do with them what you want to.

Be gentle with me, in your strong hands I trust.

I am but a fragile creature, in whom faith is a must.

Each time I give myself to this dance.

It is a leap of faith for one last chance.

Poetry in Motion (The Ballerina)

Every move she makes filled with such love and grace;

Such fierce passion for dance so visible in her face;

Her commitment so obvious in each Pirouette;

Her Batterie so very fluent from the onset;

Such effortless Flic-Flac, dedicated motion;

Her movements such poetry, graceful devotion;

She's such a sight to see;

In every way she moves me.

Grace (The Ballerina)

She carries such passion in those bright blue eyes.

Her red hair flowing down, her beauty she denies.

With parted lips she gives the camera that gaze.

When she walks into a room every man's eyebrows raise.

Such grace in motion, every move she will make.

To fall in love with her, your heart she will take.

At a distance her love lies in wait, for no man to reach.

For dance is her mistress, to no avail you may beseech.

Silent Plea (The Ballerina)

Her delicate fingers guard her whispers of pain.

They cover her mouth giving her comfort to sustain.

She finds trusting very difficult, and is never at ease.

Abruptly she'll bring a man's advances to cease.

There's fire within her, which can be controlled by no man.

She throws that passion on the dance floor, the only way she can.

So beware that fragile creature she portrays herself to be.

She's as powerful in her person, as she is her dance, you'll see.

The Storm (The Ballerina)

When autumn comes, a cold wind will follow.

The ice is ever thin, your life it will swallow.

In this season of storms of hurricane force.

You will soon find that her passion is the source.

Her fiery red hair is warning to all around.

The ground you stand with her is not sound.

Don't get too comfortable, or you will find yourself burned.

When that passion is on fire, her storms leave nothing unturned.

Beware her autumn storms.

Her fiery red hair forewarns.

Daily Struggle (The Ballerina)

In defiance of the shade, the trespassing sun beats down upon her room.

The mirror tells her there are things out of place, their fate a pending doom.

She stares at the offending clutter, so lazy in their task.

They know how it angers her, she shouldn't have to ask.

There's a place for everything, and everything should know its place.

She can feel the anger building, temperature rising, her heart begins to race.

Why must everything be such a struggle, such an impossible unnecessary fight.

They know what they're supposed to do, she restrains herself with all her might.

Beware the Season (The Ballerina)

Tread gently when she's around.

Be careful not to make a sound.

She may erupt without much reason.

It's the price you must pay, her everyday season.

You must ride the storm, if you want to be with her.

Responsibility not hers, if you hear those emotions stir.

Take them in stride, for her passion is fierce.

Take them in stride, or your heart she will pierce.

Unseen (The Ballerina)

She looks in the mirror, and sees what no one else sees.

The struggle, her wounds, the pain that just won't ease.

Her many scars she keeps hidden from the outer world she lives in.

Their judgmental gossip so detested, their glass houses thin.

She can hear them whisper every time she walks by.

They gossip to feel better, miserable lives they deny.

A strong woman is she, her passion misunderstood.

She would not change her life, even if she could.

Beautiful (The Ballerina)

Her back slightly arched, she stands before the mirror.

So beautifully formed, her dedication to her body clear.

She arouses such passion, desire, and emotion.

Her every move, gesture, and effortless motion.

In every aspect of her life, such passion pours from her skin.

Every man is tortured by her, they dream of nothing but carnal sin.

Medicinal Hue (The Ballerina)

She paints all of her walls a dark blue.

It moderates her temper, softened by the hue.

Such passion within her, pushes people away.

The soothing medicine color offers, helps her stay.

When you see the fire coming, and need to avoid the

explosion.

Simply change the color room you're in, it's not such a silly notion.

Hiding (The Ballerina)

She stands before the mirror, but must cover her face.

No one is harder on her than she is, she feels deep disgrace.

Pushing herself hard, beyond her limits, is all she's ever known.

She has sacrificed a childhood as her passion for dance has grown.

It is from the flaws she sees that she hides.

No one else sees them, the opinion collides.

Mood Ring (The Ballerina)

The little girl inside her still controls the reigns;

It is the only thing that helps keep her sane.

That little girl almost lost in a world of dedication;

She now peaks through in moments of elation.

To show she's in control, she flies her flag in High Gloss

where others find appeal.

They see that flag displayed, highlighting the perfectly formed lips they seal.

The Hair Clip she insists her adult self wear;

Must balance her mood, so others are aware.

If her mood is feeling dark, she wears bright colors to even the temper.

Her eccentric side weighs in, lighten the mood, to add a little simper.

This conflict rages on, creating such passion and beauty within her.

She wears it without apology, her fiercely independent nature.

When you see this little girl shine through.

Treat her like a rarity, be sure you do.

Passion in the Tussle (The Ballerina)

He can't resist her passion, it's what he needs above all else.

Her hair gripped tightly in his hand, he pulls passion out with a belt.

He spanks her tender buttocks, to bring the passion to the surface.

As their rapid hearts beat, their passionate tussle begins to resurface.

Their tongues pressed against each other, so passionate the kiss.

They can feel each other's heart beat, not one beat do they miss.

Her desirably delicate skin so soft against his loins.

His nerves quivering deep within, the grinding of the groins.

He probes her with his lips to find a way in.

He can't get enough of this passionate sin.

Such beauty in her form, he finds himself unnerved.

Such passionate sounds, sounds like you've never heard.

Cupid's Aggression (The Ballerina)

He grabs her so firmly, throws her on the bed.

A bed of white sheets highlighting hair, messy red.

He tears off her clothes, it can't be quick enough.

Their passion erupting, he knows she likes it rough.

The room is ice cold, but they're sweating profusely.

She yells for him to stop, but she commands him so loosely.

Blood flowing so hot, there seems no end in sight.

This heat taking such control that Cupid took flight.

Behind the Door (The Ballerina)

Leather and lace behind closed doors.

She surrenders to him the passion sores.

Out of the public eye, her persona changes completely.

She's free to let go, trusting him to punish her discretely.

Her passion is fire red, her actions stay true to that.

When the bedroom door closes, there's no judgment to combat.

It's the one time she feels free to let her guard down.

A liberating feeling, to the one who's in control about town.

Strict Consequence (The Ballerina)

Her day to day life so regimented and structured.

What no one can see, an emotional state fractured.

At arm's length, she keeps the men who desire to hold her tight.

But she needs to feel that longing as he holds her in his sight.

She desires the clasp of her hair; desires his firm grip.

Her body needs him in control, his hand on her hip.

For too long she's been missing the calloused hand of a man.

His hand on her throat, letting go, taking control like he can.

She feels the pressure of his grip.

Her clothes screaming at each rip.

That passion now flowing, her heart is pounding.

This sensation of freedom so erotic and astounding.

Freely letting go, he takes her to the ground.

These cries of passion, no more beautiful a sound.